Praise

'Kirstie has cracked the code for not-for-pre~
distilling years of experience into clear, practical
guidance. In four parts and twenty-four chapters
this book shows you how to build firm foundations,
work effectively with people, manage day-to-
day operations, govern ethically and lead with
confidence.'

> — **Mary Collin**, business coach and professional
> speaker, and Founder President, Professional
> Speaking Association (Midlands)

'In the vast forest of instructional books, occasionally
an oak tree of real achievement emerges. This is
such a book: a companion for all those who aspire to
contribute to the socially responsible world of charity
and humanistic concern for others. Let it guide your
personal journey.'

> — **Tony Drury**, founder, Earn Your Health CIC

'When you work in the not-for-profit sector, you need
to wear many hats and learn skills that your "day
job" did not train you for. This book is an essential
reference guide for those who need to know their
"unknowns"'.'

> — **Tracy Andrew**, Director T&D Consulting

'Essential reading for anyone working in a UK not-for-profit.'

— **John Field**, Director, RapportTech

'What a valuable read! Irrespective of whether you are just starting to plan a new not-for-profit enterprise or have been running one for several years and simply wish to update your skills and methodology, this book can provide the answers you need. It is clearly written, by someone with broad, varied experience who still maintains a passion for assisting and educating those people who have the heartfelt wish to enrich the lives of many, while bringing benefit to all.'

— **Paul Gardner**, retired business owner, Avonside Design

NOT-FOR-PROFIT
KNOW-HOW

Understand your responsibilities
and lead with confidence

KIRSTIE YORK

Re think

First published in Great Britain in 2025
by Rethink Press (www.rethinkpress.com)

© Copyright Kirstie York

This book is dedicated to all the amazing unsung heroes who willingly give up their time and energy to run clubs, charities, membership associations and a plethora of other not-for-profit organisations. You are a constant source of inspiration and education to me and to those around you.

Contents

Foreword

When Kirstie first told me she was writing this book, I was thrilled. I've known her for several years now through my work at Made in Britain, where her team at Cygnul delivers our administrative and customer service functions. From the outset, it was clear that Kirstie brought not only diligence and warmth but also a formidable depth of knowledge about how not-for-profits really work. That knowledge – gathered over years of supporting charities, professional bodies, and membership organisations – is what makes this book such an invaluable contribution.

Over the years, I've sat on boards, been a trustee and worked inside many not-for-profits. Here's the truth: they're far more complex than people realise. Conversations over coffee or at dinner parties have shown me again and again just how widely mis-understood not-for-profits are. To many, running a membership organisation implies posting out a few cards and throwing a dinner once a year. The reality, though, is that these organisations demand strategic thinking, financial discipline and skilled leadership, just like any other business.

First and foremost, you need to be a subject expert and a sector champion. That means engaging intelligently and passionately with members, policymakers, journalists and stakeholders, and speaking for your community with confidence and credibility.

Next comes financial stewardship, which is not just about balancing the books. It's about building reserves and investing wisely for the future. Too many organisations falter because they focus only on short-term survival rather than long-term sustainability.

Then there's strategy. We've left behind the days of 'If you build it, they will come' thinking. Today, successful not-for-profits need smart planning, clear goals and the courage to adapt. The brutal truth is that when organisations don't intelligently embrace planning, long-term strategy will flounder.

Understanding governance is equally crucial. I've seen the unpleasant mess that happens when boards confuse the requirements of Companies House with those of the Charity Commission, or when boards forget that they are both a company and a charity. That confusion can be costly, not just financially but also reputationally.

The next key element is the need to be a skilled politician. Many professional bodies and membership organisations are coalitions covering a large footprint of interests in their sector. Leadership becomes about uniting your membership around one key purpose, which takes tact, diplomacy and, above all, clarity of purpose.

Infrastructure matters too. Some organisations thrive on a spreadsheet and a simple website. Others need a fully fledged CRM, exam management systems, complex payment processing tools and a team that can deliver on every front. Knowing what your organisation needs and when is key.

Finally, there are the people. Whether it's volunteers, staff or contractors, not-for-profits need to draw on a dizzying array of skills, including those from marketers, administrators, policy experts, fundraisers, events professionals, IT specialists and more. Even if you're a leadership team of one, you'll need to understand employment law, pensions, safeguarding and right-to-work checks. It's a big ask.

There is so much that goes into running not-for-profits that this book will be a godsend for leaders, staff and volunteers alike. Kirstie has produced an essential guide that will help enhance our sector and empower many more organisations to grow.

Simon Boyd
Executive Director, Made in Britain

Introduction

This book is written for all the people who make the not-for-profit sector in the UK work. It's for the volunteers, trustees, staff and community leaders who step up to support causes they care about. Whether you're setting up a new charity, joining the committee of a community group or taking on a new staff or leadership role, this book is designed to give you the practical tools and confidence you need to do the job well.

The not-for-profit sector is incredibly diverse. While we may tend to think of charities, they are a specific subset of not-for-profit organisations. The not-for-profit sector includes professional membership associations, housing associations, sports and social clubs, volunteer-led social enterprises, specialist community-interest companies, faith-based groups, campaign movements, local networks, and more. What they all share is a commitment to public benefit and to making a positive difference in the world.

There's an idea that because you're running a not-for-profit organisation for a cause, rather than to make money, passion is more important than process. While this captures the heart of why people get involved, the legal responsibilities are real. The not-for-profit sector is no more protected from the law than those working in a profit-driven company.

Good intentions alone are not enough. Running a not-for-profit organisation requires the same skills and carries the same legal responsibilities and risks as running any other business. It requires clear governance, financial competence and strong values, along with a practical understanding of legal responsibilities, team leadership and community engagement.

The media loves attention-grabbing headlines alleging wrongdoing in not-for-profit or charitable organisations, with those reports causing untold harm to the reputation and viability of the organisations concerned. I don't want your organisation to be one of those.

In 2024 to 2025 the Charity Commission alone finalised 4,375 regulatory concern cases and used their regulatory action powers 1,858 times.[1] This figure doesn't include not-for-profit organisations who are not registered charities.

That's where this book comes in. It will demystify the basics, giving you the principles behind the regulations, answering the questions you may be afraid to ask, signposting you to the current guidance and supporting you in creating an ethical and values-driven organisation.

This book is designed to be accessible, friendly and practical, explaining key terms and focusing on what you really need to know. It is *not* a legal textbook or a substitute for professional advice, nor is it a fundraising or HR manual or an exhaustive handbook on how to run a not-for-profit. However, it will help you ask the right questions and identify when and where to seek help.

This book is structured in four parts to reflect the four pillars of not-for-profit organisations:

- **Part One: The Foundations**

    - The *why* in your vision, mission and values

    - Different legal structures and the range of not-for-profit organisations

    - What defines a charity

    - A brief history of business regulation and why it is important

- **Part Two: Working With People**

    - The different roles within an organisation

- Signposting to the legislation covering the organisation's relationship with each role

- How to nurture good working relationships through communication, collaboration and culture

- How to manage and resolve conflict

- **Part Three: Day-To-Day Operations**

  - Who you serve and what those stakeholders want or need

  - Using events to bring people together

  - Expanding impact with collaborations and partnerships

  - Sources of income, from private or government funding and grants to fundraising directly from members of the public

- **Part Four: Governance**

  - The importance of strong governance and ethical decision making by the board

  - Why meetings are legally or strategically important, and how to make them effective and inclusive

  - An overview of finance and budgets and some of the main taxes you need to be aware of

  - Your responsibilities for risk management and data protection

- Tips on data management

- How to create a culture of reflection and renewal and celebrate your achievements before looking to your next iteration

Most importantly, this book is not prescriptive. It doesn't assume one size fits all. Every organisation is different, and every reader will bring their own values, experience and context to the table.

You can read the book cover to cover, or dip in and out as needed. If you're setting up a new organisation, the early chapters on legal structure and formation will help orientate you. If you're reviewing or improving an existing organisation, you might be more focused on staffing, finance, partnerships or sustainability.

Ultimately, this book is your companion. It's here to remind you that you are not alone and to encourage you to build an organisation that is kind, courageous, transparent and effective.

PART ONE
THE FOUNDATIONS

Part One of this book is dedicated to guiding you through the legal and regulatory frameworks that support and safeguard your organisation. Understanding these basics is vital in giving your organisation the best possible start and ensuring it has the resilience to grow and thrive.

We start with your vision, mission and values. These are the practical tools that guide your decisions, inspire your community and create a shared sense of purpose. Understanding how to define and communicate them will help ensure that everyone – whether trustee, volunteer, staff member or supporter – is working towards the same goals.

From there, we turn to legal structures. Every organisation has a legal identity, and you must understand the benefits and limitations of each. The not-for-profit sector in the UK is wonderfully diverse, and with that comes a variety of ways to legally form and register your organisation. Choosing the right structure is a critical early decision that affects everything from your tax obligations to your ability to raise funds and employ staff. We'll explore the different models available, such as unincorporated associations, companies limited by guarantee (CLGs), charitable incorporated organisations (CIOs), and trusts, and help you assess what best fits your ambitions.

You will also find clarity on the differences between unincorporated associations and incorporated organisations. We'll explain the benefits and risks associated with each form and look at when it might be time to consider incorporation.

Next, we take a closer look at what makes an organisation 'charitable' in the legal sense. Registering as a charity comes with both significant benefits and responsibilities. We will help you understand whether charitable status is right for your organisation, and if so, how to register.

Finally, I'll introduce the key regulatory bodies across the UK, including Companies House, the Charity Commission (for England and Wales), Office of the Scottish Charity Regulator and the Charity Commission for Northern Ireland as well as essential topics like data protection, tax and reporting.

This part of the book is designed to give you confidence in your role and help you make informed decisions from the very beginning, avoiding common pitfalls that can hold organisations back. You will be better able to ask informed questions, seek appropriate professional advice when needed and make decisions that serve both the mission and the people behind it.

1

Understanding Vision, Mission And Values

This chapter explores how to define a clear vision, craft a compelling mission, and embed core values that guide everyday practice. We'll look at how these foundational elements shape the culture, decisions and impact of your work, helping you stay focused and connected to your cause. This chapter will also highlight the importance of alignment between values and behaviour across all levels of your organisation.

Defining your vision

The vision statement defines the organisation's core purpose – it's *why*. It should be a clear, aspirational declaration of the ideal future your organisation is working towards. For example, a group may have come together to preserve a local green space, to create a safe and welcoming place for the whole community to gather and connect. The vision should be specific but not restrictive, because it needs to inspire action and endure over time. A clear vision will help your organisation decide what activities to prioritise and to ensure funds and resources are used appropriately. While your vision is a powerful guide, it is normal for it to evolve as an organisation grows or to change completely once the original problem has been solved.

For charities, the vision must align with what's known as the organisation's *charitable purpose*. That term is defined, depending on where your charity is based, by the Charities Act 2011 (England and Wales),[2] the Charities and Trustee Investment (Scotland) Act 2005,[3] or the Charities Act (Northern Ireland) 2008.[4] You'll find more information on charitable purposes in Chapter 5.

Your vision must also demonstrate a *public benefit* – a key requirement for charitable status to be granted.

Many funders require applicants to demonstrate how their work meets specific social goals that align with the funders' priorities. If your organisation's vision is vague or overly broad, it may be more difficult to show alignment with funders' criteria. For example, if your vision is a reduction in youth unemployment, then activities like CV workshops or mentoring schemes make sense. Asking for funding to run a social club may not; you would need to clearly link the outcomes back to your goal, for example by explaining it will help young people build confidence and improve their social skills as part of their journey into work.

Whether you are crafting your first vision statement for a new group or revisiting it as part of your reflection and renewal cycle (covered in Chapter 24), the approach is similar and follows four stages:

1. **Collaboration stage.** While the process is owned and led by the board and senior leadership, it is best practice to involve a cross-section of your stakeholders. This ensures the vision will be relevant, and it encourages collective ownership.

2. **Discovery stage.** You can use surveys, interviews and workshops to explore the positive changes you want to see. Think too about what you could achieve in the long term – say, in ten to twenty years. Dream big! What will the future look like if your work makes a lasting difference?

3. **Drafting stage.** This is where you distil the shared direction into your vision statement, which should be clear and concise, expressed in one or two sentences at most. A good vision statement is aspirational, purposeful, future-focused and inclusive. It should convey the essence of your organisation, without

leaving anyone confused or having to ask for clarification.

4. **Review stage.** You should always test your statement to ensure it resonates with stakeholders and be prepared to revise and refine it before formal adoption by the board.

Identifying your mission

Once your vision is defined, it's helpful to draft a mission statement, describing your *how*. This is a concise description of what your organisation does, who the work helps and how it is done while working towards achieving your vision. It is your high-level tactical statement.

Often the vision and mission are combined into a two-part statement, so the *why* and *how* work in tandem to give a rounded view of your organisation.

Here are a few examples:

- A community arts group:
  - **Vision:** A community where creativity brings people together and everyone has the chance to express themselves.
  - **Mission:** We provide affordable workshops, exhibitions and events that make the arts accessible to all, nurturing talent and strengthening local connections.

- A youth sports club:

  - **Vision:** Every young person having the opportunity to grow in confidence and wellbeing through sport.

  - **Mission:** We offer safe, inclusive and enjoyable sporting activities, led by volunteers, that encourage teamwork, resilience and healthy lifestyles.

- An environmental friends group:

  - **Vision:** A greener, healthier neighbourhood where nature and people thrive together.

  - **Mission:** We protect and enhance local green spaces through volunteer action, education and community projects.

- An advice and support organisation:

  - **Vision:** A society where everyone can access the advice and support they need to live with dignity.

  - **Mission:** We provide free, confidential and impartial advice to local people, helping them navigate challenges and build a brighter future.

- A heritage and history society:

  - **Vision:** A community that values and celebrates its shared history.

  - **Mission:** We collect, preserve and share local stories and artefacts, engaging people of all ages in learning from the past to inspire the future.

Vision and mission statements are often used in funding applications, in annual reports, in social media bios and on organisational websites. They should be written in plain English with no jargon, buzzwords or internal acronyms. Good statements make people feel something. They invite people to believe in your work, to trust it and to get involved.

For small or volunteer-led groups, developing these statements can be a useful team-building exercise. Group members sitting down together to reflect on shared aims and aspirations can create ownership and energy.

It's also helpful to revisit your vision and mission every few years. They should evolve as your organisation grows or as the needs of your community change. However, they should never be so reactive that they lose sight of your original vision.

Embedding values and shaping culture

Values are the principles that guide how your organisation behaves. While your vision and mission statements tell people why and how you do what you do, your values express the way in which you do it. For example, is your organisation inclusive, transparent or collaborative? Do you particularly value lived experience, innovation or kindness?

Your values influence decisions across the organisation. For example, an organisation that values inclusion will think carefully about venue accessibility, representation on its board and how it gathers feedback from service users. A group that values transparency might publish its meeting minutes online or hold open forums for community members.

Values can be formally listed in your governing document or strategy, but their real power lies in how they are lived. This is where organisational culture comes in – through the shared behaviours, language and attitudes that shape your organisation's day-to-day operations.

Creating a values-based culture doesn't happen overnight. It requires intention, leadership and regular reflection. A good starting point is to involve everyone – the board, staff, volunteers, members and service users – in discussions about what matters most to your organisation. You can use a mixture of surveys and workshops to ask questions like:

- What behaviours do we admire in each other?

- What do we want to be known for?

- What are our non-negotiables in how we work?

- When are we at our best?

Another powerful technique is in providing a list of about 150 words representing different values and then asking people to narrow the list down to the top five values that they think represent the organisation.

Next, by grouping similar words or behaviours together, you can use the information gathered to identify themes and patterns. It's important not to forget to include any hidden values. These are ones you know are lived by the organisation, but because they are so deeply ingrained, they are often not overtly expressed. These might be values like honesty, fairness or compassion.

It is best to aim for between three and six core values. Once you have these, each value needs to be accompanied by a short description explaining the associated behaviours it represents. For example, I have five core values in my own business. The table below shows how I have presented each one so they are embedded in practice.

Once values are agreed, they can be woven into job descriptions, appraisals, volunteer training and team meetings. Some organisations also use values-based decision-making tools to help choose between competing priorities or navigate ethical dilemmas.

Embedding values can lead to higher trust and better morale. It also provides a benchmark for accountability, both to your community and your colleagues.

Collaboration	Teamwork Curiosity Positivity	We aim to become a valued part of our client's team. Curiosity helps us understand the motivations and drivers for the individuals and their organisation.
Stability	Responsibility Reliability Accountability Dependability	We become a trusted partner and take full responsibility for the delivery of the service. We remain fully accountable for any mistakes – no excuses.
Effectiveness	Efficiency Responsiveness Flexibility Originality Problem Solving	We take pride in delivering an efficient service. We help our clients streamline systems and processes and are open to original solutions.
Integrity	Honesty Trust Loyalty Fairness Respect	We promise absolute honesty and loyalty to our clients and will go out of our way to act in their best interests. We embrace difficult discussions and treat everyone fairly and with respect.
Playfulness	Fun Humour Warmth Openness Supportive	We build our teams and relationships on warmth, support and humour, and we encourage the confidence to make mistakes and learn from them. We take our jobs seriously but not ourselves.

Key points

- **Vision.** A vision statement is fundamental in determining your *why* – the future your organisation is working towards. It will guide long-term priorities, even as the vision statement develops over time. If you run a charity, don't forget that your vision must align with your charitable purposes.

- **Mission.** Your mission statement outlines your *how* – the ways in which your organisation is working towards its end goals. By helping others see and believe in what you are doing, your vision and mission statements can be powerful tools. Additionally, for charities, they are often crucial in applications for funding.

- **Values.** Values guide how your organisation operates, shaping your culture and influencing decision making. Once you have identified your core values, they will form the basis for your day-to-day operations, including training, appraisals and meetings. A strong values-based culture fosters trust and provides a benchmark for internal and external accountability.

2

Choosing The Right Legal Structure

The legal structure of your organisation will dictate your responsibilities in terms of liability, regulation and reporting. Understanding the differences will enable you to make confident, well-informed choices that support your organisation's goals and long-term sustainability, whether you're forming a new not-for-profit or reviewing an existing structure.

Choosing the wrong structure can leave an organisation unable to access certain funding streams or restricted in other, unforeseen ways. In addition, operating under the wrong structure, without the expected level of governance oversight, can damage the confidence of funders, partners and your community.

This chapter walks you through the main types of legal structure available to not-for-profit organisations in the UK. It also includes some examples to show the benefits of choosing the right structure and the potential pitfalls of choosing the wrong one. Because you may be joining an organisation rather than founding one, we'll also look at how to identify the structure of an existing organisation.

It's worth noting that, while it is possible to restructure, and you most often see this as part of a strategic growth plan, it can be a time-consuming process. In some cases, restructuring may mean having to close down the existing organisation and transfer assets to a new body.

Overview of legal structures

Not-for-profit organisations in the UK have a choice of several legal forms, depending on their size, activities and ambitions:

- Unincorporated association
- Community amateur sports club
- Charitable trust
- Charitable incorporated organisation
- Company limited by guarantee
- Community interest company
- Cooperative or community benefit society

Each comes with different benefits and responsibilities, as outlined here.

Unincorporated association

An unincorporated association is the simplest form. It requires no formal registration beyond a written constitution, ie the internal rules the organisation must follow, and is ideal for small, informal groups such as a neighbourhood social or sports club. However, individuals, usually committee members, are personally liable for any contracts and debts, because unincorporated associations have no separate legal identity.

Community amateur sports club (CASC)

CASCs are a special form of unincorporated association recognised by HMRC (His Majesty's Revenue and Customs). CASC status allows local sports clubs to benefit from some of the tax advantages of charity status without becoming registered charities. It is worth noting that CASCs are permitted to incorporate with Companies House at a later stage, but they must reapply for CASC status if they do this.

Charitable trust

Charitable trusts are often used to manage money or property donated for a specific purpose. Trustees are responsible for the administration of the trust and must follow the rules set out in the trust deed. Trusts are great for grant-making bodies but less flexible for charities delivering a service. Charitable trusts must be registered with the relevant Charity Commission if they meet the income threshold. At the time of writing this is £5,000 in England and Wales.[5]

Charitable incorporated organisation

A CIO is a relatively new structure, which came into force on 1 January 2013 but is available for charities only in England and Wales. It provides a legal identity and limited liability without the need to register with Companies House. CIOs report only to the Charity Commission, making administration simpler and more streamlined than the dual registration required for a charitable company.

Company limited by guarantee

A CLG is relatively common in membership associations and not-for-profits. Instead of the company being owned by shareholders, it is owned by its members, and the members act as guarantors for any debt incurred by the company. CLGs are registered with Companies House and, if charitable, also with the Charity Commission. This structure suits organisations needing a formal governance framework and the ability to enter into contracts.

Community interest company

A CIC is a limited company designed for social enterprises. CICs aim to benefit the community rather than private shareholders. They report to Companies House and must meet the community interest test administered by the CIC Regulator. Profits must be reinvested for public benefit, and there are limits on dividends and asset transfers.

Cooperative or community benefit society

Cooperatives and community benefit societies are registered with the Financial Conduct Authority (FCA). They are member-owned organisations, often used for mutual-aid or community enterprises. Cooperatives operate on the principle of one member, one vote; while community benefit societies (BenComs) aim to benefit the wider public. BenComs can also in some cases apply for charitable status.

Each structure has its own strengths, limitations and reporting requirements. The best choice of structure for your organisation will depend on your goals, your risk appetite and how formal or scalable your organisation needs to be. For example, while charities tend to be more regulated, they can generally access more funding streams, whereas social enterprises and CICs may offer greater flexibility.

Key considerations when choosing a legal structure

Choosing the best legal structure requires thinking through how your organisation will operate and grow. You may want limited liability, for example, if your group is signing contracts, renting premises or handling money, in which case you could benefit from the legal protection offered by an incorporated structure. CIOs, CLGs and CICs offer this by creating a separate legal identity, meaning that the organisation, not individual trustees, can sign contracts and hold assets.

You may want the benefits that come with charitable status. For example, it may be that you want to benefit from Gift Aid, or your preferred funder will support only registered charities. If public benefit is at the heart of your work, you might register as a CIO or CLG with charitable status. Bear in mind, however, that charity regulation comes with extra duties, including trustee responsibilities, public benefit reporting and governance requirements.

If your income will be mainly from selling services via contracts or consultancy, a CIC or social enterprise model might be more appropriate than the structure of a traditional charity. CIC and social enterprise structures can be more flexible and are not limited by charity law restrictions on political campaigning or private benefit.

Always consider how much capacity you have for administration and accountancy costs, as different structures involve varying levels of compliance and reporting. For example, a CIO may offer a lighter administrative burden than a CLG, as you only report to one regulator; but for groups wanting to start small and stay informal, an unincorporated association may suffice for a time.

Another consideration is that an unincorporated group can't own property or employ staff in its own name. If your organisation is planning to do either, incorporation is required.

This is not a decision to rush, and you should always consider taking professional advice if you are in any doubt about the best structure for your circumstances.

How to identify the structure of an existing organisation

If you're joining an existing organisation, whether as a board member, volunteer or employee, it's important to understand what legal structure the organisation has.

The best way is to ask someone within the organisation for a copy of the governing document(s). This could be a constitution, rules, club rules, trust deed, will or articles of association. As the governing documents are fundamental to the ongoing existence of an organ-isation, they shouldn't be difficult to obtain, and most organisations make them freely available. However, if you are struggling to get hold of any of the governing documents or are just curious about an organisation, you could try the following investigations.

A good starting point is to look at the name of the organ-isation. If 'Limited' or 'Ltd' comes after its name, it will be a limited liability company registered at Companies House and governed by company law. You can use the search function online at Companies House to view the full company record, including the names of current and past directors and copies of the company accounts. The articles of association can be found in the filing history, under incorporation information; they will tell you what type of limited company the organisation is, along with its objects (purpose) and decision-making requirements. The articles should also clarify if the company is a charity, but you can double-check that point on the Charity Commission website.

Both CIOs and CICs must legally add their designation to their organisation name. From there, you can search the Charity Commission website to find out more about the organisation.

While CASCs must include 'CASC' in their name, there is a slight complication in that they can be unincor-porated or incorporated. HMRC publishes a list of CASCs on the gov.uk website, but you will have to conduct a second search on Companies House to find out whether the organisation is also incorporated.

Cooperative or community benefit societies are listed on the FCA website.

If your organisation is not listed at Companies House, the Charity Commission, the FCA or on the CASC list, it is probably an unincorporated association. The only way to tell for certain is by asking to see the governing document.

Key points

- **Legal structure types.** Not-for-profit organisations can choose from a number of legal structures, including unincorporated associations, CASCs, charitable trusts, CIOs, CLGs, CICs, cooperatives and community benefit societies. Each has its own benefits and drawbacks, and it is always best to seek professional advice if you're in any doubt about what's most suitable for your organisation.

- **Legal structure implications.** The legal structure of your organisation determines your responsibilities in terms of liability, regulation and reporting. For charities, choosing the right structure can facilitate funding streams and increase stakeholder confidence.

3

Unincorporated Associations

M any sports clubs and community initiatives begin informally as unincorporated associations. This chapter explores what this means in practice, from how decisions are made to what legal standing a group has. You'll learn about the advantages of simplicity and flexibility, and the potential risks of personal liability. We'll also look at specific examples and when it might be time to consider a more formal legal structure.

This chapter is particularly relevant to small, volunteer-led groups and sports clubs. It explores what unincorporated associations are, how they operate, what risks and benefits they carry and how to draft a robust constitution. It also provides general guidance on when a group might consider becoming incorporated.

Informal structures allow people to come together quickly around a shared goal, without the need to navigate complex legal processes. These organisations may seem simple, but they still carry responsibilities, particularly when it comes to equitable decision making or managing money. The organisations are also bound by contract and common law, meaning that individuals acting on the group's behalf may take on personal legal responsibility. In practice, these organisations often operate with a bank account, a small committee of elected individuals, and a written constitution. For small-scale, local or time-limited projects, this model can work well. However, if your group grows and wants to lease property or employ staff, you may need to consider incorporation.

What is an unincorporated association?

An unincorporated association is a group of individuals working together for a common non-commercial purpose. The group is not legally separate from its members, which means it doesn't have a legal identity of its own. The organisation can't own property, enter into contracts or employ staff in its own name. Instead, these responsibilities must be taken on by individuals acting on the organisation's behalf.

Many local sports clubs, community groups and membership associations, for example, are unincorporated associations.

Unless they apply for charitable status, unincorporated associations don't need to register with Companies House or the Charity Commission. They typically operate with a written constitution, a bank account in the group's name, and a small management committee. This simplicity makes the structure attractive for grassroots initiatives, pilot projects and short-term campaigns.

The lack of a legal identity separate from the committee members has important consequences, though, because committee members may become personally liable for debts, contracts or legal claims. For example, if a group signs a hall-hire agreement for a community event and causes damage, the person who signed the contract may be held personally liable for the costs. Likewise, if the group is awarded a grant and fails to deliver the expected outcomes, individual committee members may be asked to repay the money. This means that if the group is managing substantial funds, leasing premises or employing people, it should actively consider moving to an incorporated structure.

Community amateur sports clubs

The structure of a CASC is attractive because of the charitable tax advantages without the burden of charity registration. There are strict rules on eligibility and ongoing compliance, though, which make CASC status suitable only in a narrow set of circumstances.[6] It is strongly recommended that you seek specialist advice if you are considering this option.

To qualify, a CASC must:

- Be open to the whole community

- Be organised on an amateur basis

- Provide and promote facilities for eligible sports, as listed by Sport England[7]

- Not exceed the income threshold for trading and property use[8]

Key benefits include exemption from corporation tax on trading income up to a threshold, and eligibility to claim Gift Aid on donations and business rates relief if premises are used for qualifying purposes.

Clubs must have a constitution that demonstrates compliance with the CASC rules. The governing document should include a non-profit distribution clause and a dissolution clause, and demonstrate that the club is genuinely open to all.

There are strict rules around payments to players and the use of facilities. A CASC can pay reasonable expenses but not wages to players; otherwise, it risks losing its status. HMRC guidance is detailed, and clubs should regularly review their compliance.

The constitution

The constitution is usually the governing document for an unincorporated association. While there is no legal obligation to have one, it's often required as part of a larger governing body membership requirement, for example affiliated sports clubs, or if you're applying for funding or charitable status. In addition, most banks and funding providers will ask to see it.

A well-drafted constitution outlines:

- The group's name and purpose
- Membership rules – who can join and their rights and responsibilities
- How decisions are made – eg voting rights, meetings, quorum
- Roles and responsibilities of officers
- Financial rules – eg who can sign cheques, how money is managed
- Procedures for changes to the constitution or winding up of the group

It is good practice to include in the constitution how disputes will be handled, for example with a casting vote from the chair, or by formal mediation for more serious matters, and how the group ensures transparency and fairness in decision making.

It is usual to include a clause on dissolution, ie what happens to assets if the group closes. This usually stipulates that any funds remaining after settlement of debts will be donated to another organisation or charity working in the same sector. It is unusual to identify a potential recipient by name in the document as they may not exist in the future; more common would be to leave it to the discretion of the committee in office at the time.

There are many model constitutions available, and it is recommended you use one of these templates rather than starting from scratch, to ensure you don't miss anything. You can find relevant templates at your sport's governing body, the Charity Commission, local councils for voluntary services (CVSs), Community Matters, and the National Association for Voluntary and Community Action (NAVCA), amongst others.

Ideally, the constitution should be agreed at a general meeting and reviewed at least annually. It should be treated as a living document that reflects how the group operates in practice.

Managing the risks of unincorporated associations

Risk management is crucial for unincorporated groups because of the personal liability held by committee members. You can't completely remove risk, but you can manage it.

Things to consider include:

- Good governance procedures
- Clear financial procedures
- Conflict of interest policies

In practice, this means you should hold regular committee meetings with clear agendas and minutes. You also need to ensure officers know their responsibilities, that spending is authorised and monitored by more than one person, and that there are robust conflict of interest procedures in place, with a register of conflicts reviewed regularly.

Insurance is also an important factor in mitigating risks. Public liability insurance is essential if you're organising events or using public spaces. It is also possible to purchase officers' cover insurance for the committee members, to mitigate the risk of legal action over decisions made while in post. Any good broker will be able to advise on your particular options.

While these steps help, they don't change the fact that an unincorporated association is not a separate legal entity. Incorporation is the only way to limit personal liability.

Key points

- **Overview.** The informal structure of an unincorporated association can be ideal for grassroots initiatives, pilot projects and short-term campaigns. Unincorporated associations typically operate with a written constitution, a bank account and a small management committee.

- **Benefits and risks.** Benefits include the simplicity of setup and flexibility in operations. The main risks arise from committee members being personally liable for debts, contracts and legal claims. As an organisation increases in size, therefore, incorporation should be considered.

- **Constitution and risk management.** While not legally required by an unincorporated association, a constitution is helpful in regulating operations, and it is often required in applications for funding. Good governance, clear financial procedures, conflict of interest policies and appropriate insurance are essential for managing risk.

4

Incorporated Organisations

Incorporating your organisation gives it a distinct legal identity, which can offer greater protection and credibility than with an unincorporated association. This chapter introduces the most common forms of incorporation for UK not-for-profits, including CLGs, charitable companies, CIOs and Royal Charters. We'll explain what incorporation involves and how it affects your responsibilities.

While incorporation is often the next logical step for growing unincorporated associations, you have the choice to incorporate at the point of establishment of any not-for-profit organisation.

An incorporated organisation is also known as an *artificial person*, because it is an independent legal entity that can enter into contracts, own property and be held accountable for decisions or actions carried out in its name. This protects the individuals involved from personal liability and provides funders, regulators and partners with greater confidence that the organisation is stable and professional.

Incorporated organisations are subject to more regulation and costs, but the benefits can far outweigh the increased oversight. Those benefits include:

- Increased access to funding

- Clearer governance requirements

- Reduced personal risk for those in leadership roles

The two main types of incorporated not-for-profits in the UK are CLGs and CIOs, as outlined below.

Companies limited by guarantee

A CLG is a company structure commonly used by membership organisations, charities and social enterprises. Unlike private companies with shareholders, companies limited by guarantee have members who act as financial guarantors, but the shares are not traded, ie you can't buy or sell shares in a CLG, and they have no tangible value. The members agree to pay a nominal amount – usually £1 – if the company is wound up either during their association with the company or up to twelve months after they have left. This limits liability in the event of a claim to the assets owned by the company. It also contrasts with a commercial company limited by shares, where the shares have a value that is usually based on the profitability of the company and can change depending on the current value of the company and the number of shares issued.

It's important not to confuse limited financial liability with any reduction in the responsibilities of being a director of a limited company. Company law sets out certain standards of behaviour for directors, including a requirement that they:

- Act for the good of the company

- Provide proper financial oversight

- Ensure the company acts within the powers laid out by the governing document

The directors and management committee – if they are deemed to be equally responsible for decisions and are, therefore, acting as *shadow directors* – will face scrutiny for any decisions made by the company. If an investigation finds them guilty of misconduct or negligence, a court could still find them personally liable.

Limited companies – whether limited by shares or by guarantee – are registered with Companies House and must follow company law. Companies must appoint one or more directors, who control the assets of the company and make decisions on its behalf. To act as a company director, an individual must be at least sixteen years of age and not be disqualified from acting as a director. Directors can be disqualified for unfit conduct, including:

- Not keeping proper accounting records

- Not submitting accounts and returns to Companies House

- Not paying the correct tax

- Using company money or assets for personal benefit

- Allowing a company to continue trading when it can't pay its debts

Individuals can also be prevented from acting as a director under financial restrictions after bankruptcy or a debt relief order.

Directors have their details published on the Companies House website. By law they must provide their details for the register, including home address, full date of birth and nationality. They can, however, choose to display the registered business address on the public register, and only their year of birth is published for security reasons.

In addition to the requirements listed above, the Economic Crime and Corporate Transparency Act, which became law in October 2023, was introduced to improve the quality of data on the Companies House register and enhance corporate transparency. Companies must register a valid contact email address and are no longer allowed to use a PO box as their registered address. From November 2025, to improve accuracy and reduce unlawful business activities, individuals will also undergo more robust identity checks when filing their annual confirmation statement.[9]

Charitable companies are registered with both Companies House and the Charity Commission and must abide by the rules of both. The organisation requires the appointment of trustees and directors, and it is usual for those roles to be held by the same people. Existing dual-registered charities are able to transition to a CIO, which reports only to the Charity Commission. You'll find details of the benefits of changing to CIO status at the end of this chapter.

Memorandum of incorporation and articles of association

When incorporated companies (whether limited by shares or by guarantee) are formed, they are required to submit a legal document – the *memorandum of association* – to Companies House. The memorandum simply states the company name and date of incorporation, the type of company, the act under which it is formed, the limited liability of its shareholders or guarantors and the name(s) and signature(s) of the individual(s) agreeing to form the company.

As soon as the memorandum is registered, it becomes a historical document that cannot be updated. At the same time, the company adopts its *articles of association*, which set out how decisions are made, how directors are appointed and how the organisation operates. The articles are the ongoing governing document for the company and can only be amended with a resolution at a general meeting, either the annual general meeting (AGM) or an extraordinary general meeting (EGM). The new articles must then be posted to Companies House with a copy of the signed resolution to be added to the public record.

Model (standard) articles for companies are available from Companies House.[10] While you can amend those or create your own, it is essential that articles of association contain the right, legally sound clauses. You should therefore take professional advice if you choose to do this.

I have seen sets of articles that include minute and prescriptive detail on how the organisation should be run on a day-to-day basis. This level of detail has made it almost impossible for the organisation to respond to changing circumstances without calling an EGM to change the articles. A better approach is to adopt the common practice of having an additional *members agreement* or *terms and conditions* document, which remains internal to the organisation. This sets out how the company is run on a day-to-day basis, and it can be amended much more easily, usually by a board vote.

Charitable incorporated organisations

Created specifically for charities, the status of charitable incorporated organisations (CIOs) combines the limited liability advantages of incorporation with the simplicity of single regulation by the Charity Commission. Introduced in 2013, CIO status is increasingly popular among new charities, particularly where simplicity and liability protection are priorities. The governing document for a CIO is a constitution, and no memorandum of incorporation and articles of association are needed.

CIOs must keep statutory registers and submit an annual report to the Charity Commission, which is then published on their website.

Royal Charters

Royal Charters are a particular form of company formation, distinct from a company formed under the

Companies Act. Although a Royal Charter is still a *corporate body* with its own legal identity, a Royal Charter is a formal grant from the monarch, made on the advice of the Privy Council. Originally developed to create public or private corporations (including towns and cities), they are now reserved for bodies that work in the public interest.

Instead of being formed with a memorandum and articles of association, the Charter sets out the organisation's constitution, powers and governance requirements. Amendments to their Charter must be approved by the Privy Council. A list of charters granted is published by the Privy Council.[11]

While organisations with a Royal Charter still give limited liability protection to the board, they are not limited companies in the standard sense. They will not have an entry at Companies House unless they were already a registered company prior to applying for chartered status. Chartered organisations can apply for charitable company status.

Chartered organisations are subject to the same HMRC tax obligations and benefits as other not-for-profit or charitable organisations. Chartered charities are required to follow Charity Commission reporting requirements. Non-charitable Royal Charter organisations are not obliged to publish their annual accounts, unless they are already registered with Companies House. However, many choose to include financial details in their annual reports to demonstrate their accountability to members and the public.

Key points

- **Protection from personal liability.** Incorporation creates a separate legal entity, providing protection for directors and trustees. It also increases credibility to funders, regulators and partners.

- **Different types of incorporated not-for-profits.** CLGs and CIOs are the most common forms of incorporated not-for-profits. CLGs are governed by Companies House regulation. Charitable companies are subject to dual regulation (with Companies House and the Charity Commission), while CIOs are regulated solely by the Charity Commission.

- **Companies formed by Royal Charter.** This is a special type of incorporated not-for-profit, often used by professional and public bodies. Very few new Royal Charters are granted each year. Amendments to the Charter must be approved by the Privy Council.

- **Legal and regulatory obligations.** Once a not-for-profit is incorporated, directors must abide by specific legal and regulatory obligations, including adhering to the governing documents.

5

Charitable Organisations

Charitable status is an instantly recognisable stand-ard for qualifying not-for-profit organisations in the UK. While registering as a charity brings a number of legal, financial and reputational benefits, it also comes with multiple responsibilities. As an overview, each charity must:

- Only operate services in line with its stated charitable purposes

- Serve the public benefit

- Comply with charity law

This chapter explains what makes an organisation char-itable, and it describes the different types of charities in the UK and how they are regulated. It also explores the advantages and disadvantages of becoming a charity, to show how charity status shapes day-to-day governance and accountability.

What makes an organisation a charity?

In England and Wales the legal definition of a charity is set out in the Charities Act 2011.[12] A charity must be established for exclusively charitable purposes, as recognised in law, and provide public benefit.

The thirteen charitable purposes, set out in the act and listed on the Charity Commission website, are:

1. The prevention or relief of poverty

2. The advancement of education

3. The advancement of religion

4. The advancement of health or the saving of lives

5. The advancement of citizenship or community development

6. The advancement of the arts, culture, heritage or science

7. The advancement of amateur sport

8. The advancement of human rights, conflict resolution or reconciliation or the promotion of religious or racial harmony or equality and diversity

9. The advancement of environmental protection or improvement

10. The relief of those in need, by reason of youth, age, ill-health, disability, financial hardship or other disadvantage

11. The advancement of animal welfare

12. The promotion of the efficiency of the armed forces of the Crown, or of the efficiency of the police, fire and rescue services or ambulance services

13. Any other charitable purposes – this includes any charitable purpose not covered by the other descriptions of purposes and any new charitable purposes that may be recognised in the future as being similar to another charitable purpose

The list of charitable purposes above provides a framework for understanding what activities can be considered charitable and ensures that charities operate for public benefit. This means charities must benefit a sufficiently large group of people and that any private benefit such as payment to trustees or staff must be incidental and reasonable. The Charity Commission publishes guidance on how to demonstrate public benefit, and charities must clearly explain this in their annual reports.[13]

To qualify for registration with the Charity Commission (in England and Wales), an organisation must have an annual income of over £5,000, unless it is a CIO, which must register regardless of income.

In Scotland and Northern Ireland the definitions are broadly similar, and registration is with the Office of the Scottish Charity Regulator (OSCR) or the Charity Commission for Northern Ireland (CCNI), respectively.

If a charity is operating (ie delivering services or fundraising) in more than one region of the UK, as well as registering with the regulator where it is based and complying with their reporting requirements, the charity will need to do the same with the charity regulator in each additional area.

Types of charitable organisations

Charitable organisations can take several legal forms. The most common are:

- Charitable trusts

- Charitable unincorporated associations

- Charitable incorporated organisations

- Charitable companies (usually CLGs)

- Exempt and excepted charities

Charitable trusts

One of the oldest charity structures in the UK, a charitable trust is a legal arrangement placing assets like cash, property and investments under the stewardship of trustees. Trusts are often formed through wills to leave an enduring legacy for a cause favoured by the donor.

Trusts are governed by a *trust deed* and controlled by trustees. Grant-making trusts usually distribute the income earned from investment of the underlying assets in the trust, leaving the capital to continue to grow. Because the trust has no separate legal identity, any contracts or liabilities fall to the trustees personally, unless the trust is managed under an incorporated organisation. This could be a charitable company or a CIO, where the organisation itself takes on the legal responsibilities rather than the individual trustees.

Charitable unincorporated associations

These are informal groups whose governing document is normally their constitution or rules. Occasionally the governing document may be called a scheme. Schemes are issued by the relevant Charity Commission to create, amend or clarify the rules. Charitable unincorporated associations do not have a separate legal identity, so the trustees are personally liable for entering into contracts.

Charitable unincorporated associations are particularly suitable for small, local or volunteer-led charities that do not employ staff. However, due to their small and informal structures, they may face challenges when applying for larger grants, entering into leases or employing staff as they grow.

Charitable incorporated organisations

The CIO legal structure is particularly attractive to small and medium-sized charities that want to avoid dual reporting. CIOs have a separate legal identity from the trustees, which provides limited liability, and CIOs only need to register with the Charity Commission, not Companies House, making the reporting burden lighter. Scotland offers a structure similar to that of a CIO but the facility is not available in Northern Ireland.

There are two main types of CIO:

1. **Foundation CIOs** – run by trustees only, without a wider membership

2. **Association CIOs** – run by trustees and other members who can vote on governance matters

The governing document for a CIO is its constitution, which must follow one of the model forms approved by the Charity Commission.[14] These include detailed provisions on trustee powers and duties, membership rights and responsibilities (for association CIOs), quorums, voting procedures, conflict of interest policies and processes for amendment of the constitution or dissolution of the CIO.

Charitable companies (usually CLGs)

These are incorporated organisations that register with both Companies House and the Charity Commission. They are suitable for larger or more complex operations and provide legal identity and limited liability. This structure is widely recognised and accepted by funders, lenders and statutory agencies. The dual reporting, however, involves additional administration.

Exempt and excepted charities

Some charities are exempt from registering with the Charity Commission because they are regulated by another body.[15] This is often the case with universities, further education colleges and some housing associations. Others are excepted due to their size or nature; for example, certain church denominations or Scout and Guide groups that operate under a specific income threshold.[16] These charities must still comply with charity law but may not appear on the public register of charities.

Regulation, governance and reporting

All UK-registered charities are regulated by one or more of the three charity regulators:

1. Charity Commission (England and Wales)

2. OSCR (Scotland)

3. CCNI (Northern Ireland)

These regulators ensure charities operate within their charitable purposes, demonstrate public benefit, submit annual reports and accounts, and abide by suitable governance and safeguarding practices.

In England and Wales charities with an income over £25,000 must submit an annual return. Those with an income over £250,000 must submit accruals-based accounts and may need an independent examination or audit, depending on income and asset thresholds. Smaller charities still need to keep accurate records and report income and expenditure appropriately.

Trustees are responsible for ensuring compliance. They must always:

- Act in the charity's best interests

- Manage assets and resources responsibly

- Comply with the law and the charity's governing document

- Avoid conflicts of interest

- Declare all relevant interests

It is good practice for all new trustees to undertake induction and training. Free resources are available through the Charity Commission, National Council for Voluntary Organisations (NCVO), Scottish Council for Voluntary Organisations (SCVO) and other sector bodies. Trustees can be held personally liable if they act dishonestly or negligently, so it is vital the charity makes sure trustees fully understand their responsibilities.

Key points

- **Legal definition and requirements.** To register as a charity in the UK, an organisation must have exclusively charitable purposes and provide a public benefit. It must also operate according to the rules outlined in its governing document and comply with charity law.

- **Structures.** There are five main types of charitable organisation in the UK, all with distinct legal structures, liabilities and reporting obligations.

- **Regulation.** Charities are regulated by the Charity Commission (England and Wales), OSCR (Scotland) or CCNI (Northern Ireland), which ensure any charity operates lawfully and effectively for the public good.

6

The History Of Regulation

The number one thing I want readers of this book to understand is that in regard to business regulations, running a not-for-profit is the same as running any other business. Whatever the size or structure of an organisation – unincorporated or incorporated – you still take on the same legal, financial and ethical responsibilities as those working in the private sector.

This chapter provides an overview of your obligations to Companies House, charity regulators, the Crown (via the Privy Council), HMRC and the Information Commissioner's Office (ICO), most of which require some form of submission each year and have legal powers to enforce their requirements. It also gives a little of the history of how each organisation was formed and why.

Companies House

Companies house was first established by the government through the Joint Stock Companies Act 1844, with the hope that a central register of legitimate companies would help to protect members of the public from fraud.[17] A revision to the act in 1856 provided limited liability protection for shareholders, while introducing the requirement for evidence that the company was legitimately trading, in the form of the submission of memoranda and articles of association as well as annual reports. Companies House went on to become an official executive agency of the British Government, ie administratively separate but still part of the government, in 1988.

It is worth noting that Companies House acts as a regulator rather than an enforcer. Its main focus is to ensure the availability and accessibility of public data, but it cannot police the behaviour of directors or oversee the governance of companies.

Companies House holds the public register of limited companies in the UK and is responsible for incorporating all companies within England, Scotland and Northern Ireland. There are in fact three public registers – one for England and Wales, one for Scotland and one for Northern Ireland. Due to the different legal systems in each area, your organisation must be separately registered within each jurisdiction in which it carries out activities.

The public register of limited companies is available via the Companies House website and contains the following information for each limited company:

- Name of the company, plus any previous names or trading names

- Unique company registration number

- Date of incorporation

- Address of registered office

In addition, the name, date of birth (month and year only) and dates of appointment and resignation are shown for every officer (director or company secretary) associated with the company. To show the full history of the company and any associated individuals, officers' names are not removed from the register.

Companies House also records details of any *persons with significant control* (PSCs). In the case of a commercial company, this will be the owner or shareholders, but PSC is less likely to apply in not-for-profit companies where no shares are issued. Sometimes you will see the chair listed as the sole PSC, but this is not necessary in organisations where board members have equal voting rights.

If the company owns property, details of any mortgages or charges are recorded in the public register. When due diligence checks are conducted on any company,

any insolvency is also important information, and this is also recorded on the register.

Responsibilities

Legally, you must tell Companies House about any changes to your company's information – including change of address, officer appointments or resignations and contact details – within fourteen days of the change occurring. Companies House data is widely used and trusted by banks, regulators, funders, researchers, journalists and members of the public. In the 2023–2024 financial year the register was accessed over sixteen and a half billion times.[18]

Key filing dates:

- Annually, you must file copies of your accounts with Companies House, and you will receive an automatic penalty notice if this is not done within nine months of the financial year end.

- The associated corporation tax must be calculated and paid within nine months and one day of the financial year end.

- Confusingly, the company's tax return must be filed within twelve months of the financial year end. In practice, though, your company accountant will usually file the accounts and tax return at the same time.

- You must file an annual confirmation statement within fourteen days of the anniversary of incorporation, verifying that the details held by Companies House, including those not in the public domain, are up to date and accurate.

Late filing of any documents and information may result in a penalty. Details of the current penalties can be found on the Companies House website.[19]

Following the introduction of Part 13 of the Companies Act 2006, which came into effect on 1 October 2007, private companies, that is, companies whose shares are not traded on the stock market, are no longer required by Companies House to have their accounts presented to members at an AGM.[20] They are not even required to hold a general meeting, as long as annual accounts are sent to members. However, you must check what your articles state, as they are your overarching governing documents. As it used to be a requirement, many organisations still present accounts to members at the AGM for agreement prior to submission to Companies House, and they must continue to do so unless their articles are changed to remove that requirement.

Charity regulators

There are three charity regulators in the UK and Northern Ireland:

1. Charity Commission

2. OSCR

3. CCNI

Charity Commission

Similar to Companies House, the Charity Commission can trace its roots back to a time of increasing public concern about the misuse of charitable funds. The Charitable Trusts Act 1853 was the first step towards charity regulation, leading to formation of the Charity Commission, although at that time it had limited powers and focused primarily on auditing and advising.

It was the Charities Act 1960 that introduced a central register of charities and gave the Charity Commission greater powers to investigate misconduct. The Charities Act 2006 went even further, introducing the 'public benefit' test and the added legal structure of CIO.

As of March 2025, the Charity Commission regulated more than 170,000 registered charities in England and Wales.[21]

OSCR

The OSCR was established following the devolution of powers to the Scottish Parliament on 1 July 1999. This laid the foundations for the Charities and Trustee

Investment (Scotland) Act 2005, with the OSCR being formally established in 2006.

As of 2025, OSCR regulates more than 25,000 charities operating in Scotland.[22]

CCNI

The Charities Act (Northern Ireland) 2008 set the groundwork for the CCNI, but its full launch was delayed until 2013. As of 2025 it regulates more than 7,000 charities.[23]

Responsibilities

As well as providing guidance and support to charities, each of these charity regulators has powers to ensure compliance and investigate concerns. While the rules are similar across all three bodies, they are not identical. Trustees must make themselves aware of the specific requirements of the body where their charity is registered and/or operates. Annually, the charity is expected to provide an annual report and accounting information, as well as reporting any changes to its trustees and governing documents.

The Privy Council

The Privy Council is one of the oldest institutions of British government, with origins in the Norman kings' (1066–1154) inner circle of advisers.[24] In the early centuries it wielded broad political and judicial powers, but as government departments and the courts evolved, most of these functions were delegated. What remains is a set of historic and constitutional duties, among them the granting and amendment of Royal Charters. In medieval and early modern times, charters were used to incorporate cities, universities, guilds and trading companies. The earliest recorded Charter is the Weavers Company on 17 November 1155.[25] The Privy Council continues to grant charters and oversee existing chartered corporations, performing a role similar to Companies House.

There are approximately 700 members of the Privy Council, although only a handful are involved in active business at any one time. Membership is for life and members are appointed by the monarch on the advice of the Prime Minister. By convention, those invited to join include Cabinet ministers and senior politicians, senior judges of the Court of Appeal and the UK Supreme Court, certain bishops of the Church of England, and occasionally members of the Royal Family or other distinguished individuals.

For Royal Charter matters, business is conducted by a small working group of Privy Counsellors – usually current ministers and senior officials.

Responsibilities

The Privy Council will formally consider requests for amendments to existing Charters and petitions for new applications. If approved, decisions are issued as Orders in Council. This ensures that changes to the constitutions of professional institutes, charities, universities and other chartered bodies are subject to proper constitutional scrutiny, rather than being altered solely by the organisations themselves.

In this way, the Privy Council maintains an important regulatory function. It provides continuity between historic incorporation by Royal Charter and the demands of modern governance, ensuring that institutions holding charters remain accountable to the Crown and, by extension, to the public interest.

HMRC

Although the practice of using customs officers to levy taxes on trade dates back to the medieval period, the Board of Customs was established in the seventeenth century to collect taxes on goods that were imported or exported. The Board of Excise followed in the early eighteenth century, to raise taxes on goods produced or used within the UK, like the current duties on fuel and alcohol. HM Customs and Excise itself was formalised as a body in 1909 through the merger of the Board of Customs and the Board of Excise.

The Inland Revenue was formed in 1849 to centralise the collection of direct taxes like income tax, property taxes and stamp duty, with the date reflecting the shift to waged employment in the newly built cities from the previous rural subsistence farming and barter economy.

In April 2005 the Inland Revenue and HM Customs and Excise merged to form HMRC under the Commissioners for Revenue and Customs Act 2005, to streamline services and improve efficiency. HMRC is a non-ministerial department that reports to Parliament through the Treasury.

Responsibilities

In relation to businesses, HMRC is responsible for the collection of taxes and the administration of certain regulatory regimes such as the national minimum wage and some anti-money laundering activities. Registered organisations are issued a unique tax reference (UTR) number, which must be used in all correspondence with HMRC. Common taxes and reliefs that may apply to your organisation are PAYE (pay as you earn), corporation tax, VAT (value-added tax) and Gift Aid.

Data protection and the ICO

The first iteration of the ICO was established in conjunction with the Data Protection Act 1984, which itself was passed in response to concerns over how personal information was being collected, stored and used with the advent of computers in the workplace.

With the introduction of the Data Protection Act 1998, the position of Data Protection Registrar was renamed the Data Protection Commissioner. The current name of Information Commissioner's Office was adopted in 2001 when the Freedom of Information Act 2000 expanded the role significantly, followed by adoption of the Environmental Regulations Act 2004.

The ICO is a non-departmental public body led by the Information Commissioner, who is an independent individual appointed directly by the Crown.

Responsibilities

Organisations processing personal data must register with the ICO and pay an annual fee to help fund its work.

Most recently the ICO has supported the introduction of the General Data Protection Regulation (GDPR), which came into law on 25 May 2018 and is read alongside the new Data Protection Act 2018.

The ICO has powers to conduct investigations and issue penalties for breaches of the Data Protection Act 2018. It can also issue compulsory audit notices to organisations considered to be at significant risk of compromising personal data but who refuse to cooperate.

Key points

- **Legal responsibilities.** Not-for-profits have essentially the same legal and financial obligations as private sector businesses, including annual financial submissions and compliance with regulatory bodies.

- **Regulation.** Charities are subject to regulation by charity regulators (Charity Commission, OSCR and CCNI) in addition to that of HMRC and the ICO. Some charities must also comply with Companies House legislation.

PART TWO
WORKING WITH PEOPLE

In Part Two we explore the practicalities and nuances of working with people. I'll begin with the management board, sometimes referred to as the board of directors or trustees. The board holds ultimate responsibility for the governance and strategic oversight of your organisation. Chapter 7 explores the board's roles and responsibilities, tips on effective recruitment and induction, and how to plan for succession and continuous improvement.

From there we turn to volunteers, considering legal obligations and how to create an environment where volunteers feel valued, supported and able to give their best.

Chapter 9 offers a clear introduction to employment responsibilities, including recruitment, fair and inclusive employment policies, and good supervision.

Chapter 10 looks at supporting people and managing conflict, which might include performance issues, grievances or signs of burnout. I'll outline practical strategies for supervision, support and conflict resolution, plus what to do if problems escalate.

I've also included guidance on working with contractors and why you might engage them to deliver a particular project or service. Chapter 11 explains when to use a contractor, how to find and engage the right one, how to manage the relationship professionally, and what to do if problems arise.

Finally, we look into communication, collaboration and organisational culture. Chapter 12 will help you strengthen both internal and external communication, foster teamwork and align your organisational culture with your core values.

7

The Management Board

This chapter explores the role of the board, what makes an effective director or trustee, and how to build a board that reflects your community and values.

Every not-for-profit organisation, from the smallest community group to the largest national charity, needs a group of people responsible for its operation and governance. This group may be called the board, management committee, council or trustees, but I will refer to them here as the management board or board.

The management board is responsible for the organisation's strategy, finances, legal compliance and reputation. An effective board gives clarity, accountability and leadership.

Board roles and responsibilities

The board is the governing body of an organisation. In the case of a registered company, these individuals, whether formally appointed or not, may also be acting as directors under company law. If the organisation is a registered charity, its board members are known as trustees.

The board's key role is to provide strategic direction for the organisation while maintaining oversight of its activities and performance. This includes:

- Setting the vision and mission

- Reviewing and approving key plans

- Ensuring resources are managed ethically and effectively

- Protecting the organisation's assets – not just its financial assets but also its reputation, people and intellectual property

The board is also legally responsible for making sure the organisation meets its regulatory obligations, including those related to financial reporting, safeguarding, health and safety, and data protection.

While there may be a number of roles specific to the work of your organisation, there are three key board roles that most organisations will require:

1. Chair

2. Treasurer

3. Secretary

The responsibilities of each of these roles are rooted in company and charity law, good governance and practical necessity. Differences between the three roles are outlined below.

Chair

The chair holds a position of leadership and facilitation. Their primary role is to ensure that the board functions well, with clarity, accountability, and a shared sense of purpose. According to the Charity Governance Code, the chair is responsible for leading the board and ensuring it governs effectively.[26] The NCVO recommends that boards conduct regular performance reviews of individual trustees, including the chair, each year.[27]

The chair will often be the public face of the organisation in formal settings and speak on behalf of the board at AGMs or in meetings with funders and regulators. A skilled chair works collaboratively with senior staff and volunteers to support tactical planning and performance oversight, without stepping into operational management. They provide what is often called constructive challenge, which involves asking good questions, offering guidance and ensuring the board is not simply rubber-stamping decisions. They also take responsibility for the board's development, including succession planning, diversity, skills balance and induction for new board members.

Treasurer

Legally, all board members are jointly and severally responsible for the organisation's finances. The treasurer has specific responsibility for ensuring that the board properly understands and oversees the organisation's finances. Their primary duties include:

- Presenting financial reports at board meetings in a clear and accessible way

- Explaining what the figures mean

- Ensuring that financial risks are properly managed

They might also lead on the preparation of budgets and forecasts and liaise with the accountants or auditors. In smaller organisations the treasurer may also keep financial records, monitor bank accounts and process payments.

The treasurer takes the lead in ensuring compliance with financial regulations, including submitting annual accounts to Companies House or the Charity Commission (depending on the organisation's legal structure). They should also ensure that the organisation is meeting any grant or funder reporting requirements, which is a critical part of ensuring long-term trust and funding.

Secretary

The role of secretary – sometimes known as the company secretary, particularly in organisations registered with Companies House – is often underestimated, yet it is absolutely central to good governance, smooth operations and legal compliance.

The secretary plays an important role in helping the board comply with legal and constitutional requirements. That might include checking that:

- Meetings are quorate, ie have enough people present to make decisions
- Conflicts of interest have been properly declared
- Certain decisions require member approval

They may also be responsible for submitting statutory returns such as the annual confirmation statement to Companies House or annual returns to the Charity Commission.

Traditionally, the secretary is responsible for organising meetings and ensuring that agendas are prepared, papers are circulated in advance and minutes are accurately recorded and stored. Clear and accurate minutes provide a record of decisions, action points and accountability, which are vital if a decision is ever scrutinised by a funder or regulator.

The secretary is often the person who makes sure that policies are in place and regularly reviewed and updated, and stored where people can access them. In some organisations the secretary also acts as the first point of contact for queries from regulators, members or the general public.

In practice, the role of secretary varies depending on the size and structure of the organisation. In smaller charities or community groups, the secretary might also handle correspondence, manage membership records and support the chair in preparing for the AGM. In larger organisations, many of these tasks may be delegated to staff, but the secretary should retain oversight.

Board composition, diversity and induction

A strong board is built on diversity, not just of background and identity but also of skills, experiences and perspectives. Boards benefit enormously when they include people who understand the communities they serve and can bring lived experience of the organisation's work or contribute insights from a range of sectors and life experiences.

This might mean welcoming people of different ages, ethnicities, genders, sexual orientations and faiths. It also involves being inclusive of those with disabilities, those who have used the organisation's services and people from underrepresented communities. While technical expertise in finance, law or HR is specifically required for some board roles, it is equally important to have board members who understand the organisation's impact on the ground.

Recruitment

To attract the right mix of people, the recruitment process needs to be open and transparent. Roles should be advertised with a clear description of the organisation, the individual role, the time commitment and any particular skills or experiences sought. Interview panels should be welcoming and inclusive and offer applicants the opportunity to ask questions and learn about the organisation's culture.

Induction

When new members join the board, a well-planned induction can make a big difference in how quickly they can effectively contribute and how engaged they become with the organisation. New members should be provided with an induction pack that includes key documents such as the governing document, latest accounts and strategic plan, as well as a list of board members, meeting dates, and key staff and contact points.

It can be helpful to include policies on safeguarding, conflict of interest, data protection and financial management, but the aim is to produce an easily accessible quick-start guide to instil confidence and enthusiasm, not something full of irrelevant information that will take weeks to read.

In addition, the induction might include a welcome meeting with the chair or CEO, the chance to shadow a meeting or meet frontline staff, or a buddying arrangement with a more experienced board member. Encouraging ongoing training and development such as attending webinars, workshops and relevant networking groups can help board members stay confident and informed.

Succession planning

One common risk for not-for-profits is board fatigue. When the same individuals stay on the board for years without renewal or reflection, burnout or complacency can arise, resulting in stagnation and even governance failure if practices are not updated in line with emerging threats. To avoid this, organisations should adopt term limits, for example allowing trustees to serve up to two terms of three years, which encourages fresh perspectives and gives people a natural exit point. It also allows organisations to plan ahead, identify gaps in experience and strategically recruit new members.

Undertaking a skills audit to map each board member's skills against the organisation's needs can help in spotting areas for the development of the board. Self-assessment surveys or structured conversations can further help the board to reflect on its performance, culture and areas for improvement.

Succession planning should also apply to board leadership roles, with the chair and treasurer not serving indefinitely. Organisations should develop a clear plan for handover, where appropriate including mentoring and shared leadership, which ensures continuity while allowing the development of fresh ideas.

Key points

- **The role of the board and its members.** The management board is legally responsible for ensuring legal and financial compliance and protecting the organisation's assets. Key roles include the chair, treasurer and secretary.

- **Composition, diversity, development and succession planning.** Diverse backgrounds and perspectives, structured inductions and training, and fixed terms for each role contribute to the strength of the board and encourage fresh ideas. A skills audit is important in identifying each board member's skills and areas for improvement and contributes to effective succession plans.

8

Working With Volunteers

This chapter looks at the legal, practical and emotional aspects of engaging volunteers, from recruitment and onboarding to ongoing support and recognition. You'll learn how to create a positive volunteer experience while addressing potential challenges like boundaries and conflict. We'll also explore the importance of valuing volunteer contributions and building a culture of mutual respect.

Volunteers and the law

Volunteers are not the same as paid employees, and this legal distinction has important implications. Unlike employees, volunteers do not have a contract of employment and are not entitled to employment benefits such as pay, paid holidays or pension contributions.

It is vital not to blur the lines between volunteers and employees, as there could be consequences for both the individual and the organisation. If a court decided your agreement constituted a contractual employee relationship, you could become liable for paying at least national minimum wage, which would have implications for the individual in terms of taxation and benefits, as well as an impact on your organisation's financial situation.

Volunteer health and safety and safeguarding responsibilities

The Health and Safety at Work etc. Act 1974 applies to all people affected by an organisation's work, including volunteers.[28] This means risk assessments must be carried out for volunteer activities, particularly if they involve manual handling, public engagement or working with vulnerable individuals. Adequate training, appropriate equipment and supervision should be provided to minimise the risk of harm.

Safeguarding legislation must also be considered, and it is important to have clear safeguarding policies and to ensure volunteers understand their responsibilities. Volunteers who have unsupervised contact with children or vulnerable adults need to undergo a Disclosure and Barring Service (DBS) check. This check must be proportionate to the role, though, and used only when legally appropriate.

Recruitment

Recruiting volunteers begins with being clear about what roles are needed. A good volunteer role description helps set expectations, explaining:

• What the volunteer will do

• What the volunteer should not do

• How much time the role might take

• What support is available

It should also clearly set out the standards of behaviour that are expected while the volunteer is associated with the organisation. This clarity helps people decide whether they will be a good fit for the role and reduces the risk of misunderstandings later on.

Equality legislation also applies to volunteer recruitment and management. Organisations must not discriminate on the basis of age, disability, gender reassignment, marriage or civil partnership, pregnancy or maternity, race, religion or belief, sex or sexual orientation.[29] Recruitment should be inclusive and efforts made to remove barriers to participation, including offering roles with flexible hours, providing access adaptations and valuing lived experience alongside formal skills.

Methods of advertising (or making people aware of) vacancies range in cost and effectiveness. The response you get will depend on a number of factors, including how well you define the role, write the copy and choose the right channels to advertise.

The recruitment process should be warm and respectful. It may include informal chats, application forms or trial sessions. Where roles involve sensitive responsibilities, a structured selection process may be appropriate, for example arranging interviews and securing references for volunteers supporting vulnerable people. Even informal roles benefit, though, from thoughtful matching and clear communication.

While a volunteer agreement may be used, it must not include language that implies a contractual relationship. Terms such as *job description*, *wages*, or *working hours* must be avoided. Instead, the document should be framed as a mutual understanding, outlining what the volunteer can expect, such as support, relevant training and reimbursement of expenses, and what the organisation hopes the volunteer will contribute. Otherwise, courts could decide that the volunteer has employment rights due to clauses contained within their volunteer agreement, as has happened in a small number of cases.[30]

Onboarding and supervision

Various aspects lead to the successful new start of volunteers at any not-for-profit organisation, including:

- Onboarding
- Induction
- Learning and development
- Review

Onboarding

Once a volunteer joins the organisation, a structured onboarding process is crucial. This includes:

- Welcoming the new volunteer
- Introducing them to the team
- Explaining the organisation's vision, mission and values
- Offering a tour of the space for physical premises
- Telling the new volunteer who to contact with questions
- Showing them how to record expenses
- Offering copies of key policies

Induction

The induction plan should contain a comprehensive list of what you want the volunteer to learn and how you want them to adapt current skills to deliver particular aspects of the service. Share this plan with the volunteer and give them a copy so they can record their progress independently or raise concerns about items they need more training on or support with.

It is also good to have timescales attached to each aspect of the plan so all involved can see their expected progress and what steps the organisation is putting in place to develop the volunteer. This is intended to be reassuring for them, so they can see when they are progressing as expected, but it must be realistic and adaptable so as not to cause overwhelm if progress is slower than anticipated.

Learning and development

While your volunteer development will usually cover on-the-job learning from other volunteers or staff, it will often include an element of formal learning. For a sports club this might be a formal coaching qualification or a safeguarding or first aid certificate. It could also involve attending workshops or other group training within or outside of the organisation.

As you don't have a contractual arrangement with your volunteer, it is very difficult to insist they attend training sessions. You should explain why the particular training is important for the role they wish to undertake and try to arrange session times and locations with as much flexibility as possible.

If training is compulsory for a particular role and your volunteer refuses to undertake that training, you are within your rights to move the volunteer to a role that does not require those qualifications. For example, where a sporting body mandates that lead coaches hold a particular level of qualification or a first aid certificate, an unqualified volunteer would not be able to hold that title or run sessions alone but could still support a fully qualified coach.

You should always try to match a volunteer with a role that is suitable for them and which they agree would be of interest. For example, you may have an accountant who wants to volunteer as a sports coach. While you may need a treasurer on the board, if the volunteer does not agree to fulfil this role, you can't force them to join the board or take on both roles.

Review

As with any team, it is important that both performance and wellbeing are monitored as one can have an impact on the other, just as it can with paid employees. Most people will open up about issues to their line manager as long as the questions are asked confidentially, in a friendly and supportive manner, and if there is a culture of trust within the organisation.

Supporting, recognising and retaining volunteers

Volunteers welcome support from the organisation, and that support is important in helping them to feel valued and respected. Main types of support that might be needed are:

- Financial support
- Emotional support
- Recognition

Financial support

The cost of volunteering, for example travel costs and childcare, can be a barrier for many people. Paying out-of-pocket expenses to volunteers for travel, subsistence or necessary purchases can help enormously. Expenses must be reimbursed at face value and on production of a receipt. Reimbursing more than the volunteer spent or paying a flat cash allowance could be considered payment for employment. For travel by car, the authorised mileage rates are set by HMRC.

Emotional support

Emotional support might be provided by offering debriefs after challenging experiences, creating a buddy system for new volunteers or making space for informal social connection. Volunteers who feel part of something bigger are more likely to stay and give generously of their time and skills.

Recognition

This is a key part of volunteer management. Recognition might be as simple as a personal thank you at the end of a shift or as elaborate as an annual celebration event for all volunteers. Some organisations use newsletters or social media to spotlight individual volunteers. Others offer opportunities for progression such as becoming a volunteer coordinator or contributing to project planning.

Retention

Retention of volunteers is important both for operational efficiency and for financial reasons. A high turnover results in precious time and money being spent on recruitment and induction that could be devoted to service delivery. Good retention practice starts with understanding why people volunteer in the first place. The NCVO 2023 'Time Well Spent' study reports that volunteers said their top reason for volunteering was wanting to improve things or help people.[31] They also said that making a difference was the key reason they were likely to continue. When these motivations are understood and nurtured, volunteers are more likely to stay.

Retention is also about enabling people to leave on good terms and with a sense of pride. Exit interviews and informal goodbyes provide a chance to thank volunteers for their contribution, and to reflect and understand their reasons for leaving.

Dealing with problems and complaints

While the majority of experiences of running a charitable organisation will be positive, you need to know how to handle problems. The NCVO recommends having a problem-solving process (distinct from an employee disciplinary and grievance procedure), including a document that explains what steps the organisation or volunteer should follow.

The document should include what is considered to be a problem, including allegations of serious misconduct, and could reflect the wording of the volunteer agreement in terms of expected behaviour. It should detail who has responsibility for dealing with different types of complaints and document the steps in the process, from raising a concern to making a decision and informing the complainant. It also needs to be clear on how a decision can be appealed if necessary. The NCVO provides further guidance on its website: www.ncvo.org.uk.[32]

Rember that you must not use any language that could imply volunteers are being treated like staff. A formal disciplinary procedure is tied to the legal rights of employees and is not applicable to volunteers. Equally, you cannot use employment sanctions like verbal and written warnings or dismissal with a volunteer.

You can offer advice and support to help a volunteer improve, and issues should be documented with a *note of concern*. If the issues persist then the organisation may end the volunteering agreement or ask the volunteer to step down.

Key points

- **The difference between volunteers and employees.** While you need to meet legal obligations around health and safety, safeguarding and equality in the same way as in paid employment, it is important to avoid wording in volunteer agreements that implies any employee relationship, to prevent contractual obligations for your organisation.

- **From onboarding to retention.** A number of aspects in the recruitment of new volunteers – role descriptions, the onboarding and induction processes, training, recognition and support – can lead to increased satisfaction for the new volunteer and higher retention levels.

- **Problem solving.** There will be times when problems arise in your not-for-profit. Establishing clear processes before any challenging situation occurs will be beneficial in achieving a successful outcome.

9
Employing Staff

As your organisation grows, you may reach a point where paid staff become essential. This chapter explains what's involved in becoming an employer, from legal responsibilities to creating a supportive workplace culture. We'll look at recruitment, supervision and how to ensure fair and inclusive practices. We also explore the balance between managing staff performance and supporting wellbeing.

Becoming an employer

Employing staff requires careful preparation, including around:

- Planning
- Remuneration and tax
- Practicalities

Planning

Before advertising a role, organisations must consider:

- What tasks need undertaking in the role

- Whether the role is genuinely necessary and sustainable

- How the paid role will be funded

This exercise should be revisited every time you replace a paid member of the team, because roles evolve over time and you may not need a like-for-like replacement.

Some charities employ staff to provide administrative support, while others use staff to deliver frontline services, lead projects or develop fundraising. Your initial planning for the role will shape every part of the employment journey.

Remuneration and tax

Once the decision to recruit has been made, the organisation must register as an employer with HMRC. This allows the organisation to operate PAYE, the system used to collect income tax and national insurance contributions from employees. Employers must also comply with auto-enrolment pension requirements unless a more generous provision is offered.

Don't forget to include *employer on-costs* in your staffing budget. These are additional taxes or contributions made by the employer on top of any salary deductions from the employee. They include employers' national insurance contributions and employer pension contributions.

There may be other taxes to take into account if you plan to offer significant non-cash benefits like a company car or private health insurance. In this case you should consult your accountant or payroll specialist before finalising your budget.

Practicalities

Employing someone also means considering practical arrangements. Helpful questions include:

- Will they work in a shared office, from home or in the community?

- What equipment will you need to provide, eg a phone, laptop or safety equipment?

- How will you provide training, manage their workload and review their performance?

These questions must be addressed early on so all considerations can be included in the budget to ensure a smooth start for the employee on their first day.

Recruitment, induction and supervision

Before advertising the role, it is essential to prepare a detailed job description and person specification. These documents outline what the role involves and what kind of person the organisation is looking for. As well as being used to advertise the role, job descriptions also help the organisation assess applications fairly and consistently. They should describe:

- Job title

- Working conditions

- Core duties

- Responsibilities

- Reporting lines

- Required qualifications or experience

- Preferred qualifications or experience

Use clear and inclusive language to help attract a wide range of candidates.

Fairness

Recruiting fairly is both good practice and a legal duty. The recruitment process should be open, transparent and consistent, and advertising via multiple routes helps reach a broader pool of candidates.

Offering alternative application formats is good practice, and including statements that show a genuine commitment to equality, diversity and inclusion signals that you value people of all backgrounds and abilities.

When it comes to considering your list of applicants, the following points are all important:

- Shortlisting should be based on clear, pre-agreed criteria from the person specification.

- Applications should be assessed consistently, and reasons for shortlisting (or not) should be documented.

- Interviews need to be structured and fair. Many organisations find value in having a panel of at least two people, using set questions for consistency, with an agreed scoring matrix to allow later comparison of candidates.

- Offering adjustments for disabled applicants, such as alternative interview formats, early or late slots or extra interview time, is good practice and often a legal requirement.

Some organisations also ask candidates to complete a practical task relevant to the role, for example a short writing exercise, a presentation or production of a project plan. This can offer additional insight into the candidates' skills and thinking. It is also increasingly common for applicants with lived experience in the organisation's area of work – for example of homeless-ness, disability or the criminal justice system – to be valued for the perspectives they bring to staff teams.

Job offer and contract

Once you have chosen your preferred candidate, you need to proceed to a formal job offer, in writing. This should include the headline terms of employment such as salary, job title and hours and place of work; plus any conditions on the employment offer, for example satisfactory references and pre-employment screening checks. Once the candidate has accepted your offer in principle, you can conduct your pre-employment checks and then confirm a start date.

Legally, you must issue a formal contract of employ-ment before or on the first day of work at the latest. In practice, many organisations issue the contract and handbook at the time the offer is confirmed, which allows the candidate to raise any potential issues before they commit.

The contract must include essential information like job title, hours of work, rate and frequency of pay, employ-ment start date, holiday entitlement, any probationary period, notice period, place of work, and policies for disciplinary and grievance procedures. Using tem-plates from reliable sources such as Acas (Advisory, Conciliation and Arbitration Service, www.acas.org.uk)

or an HR consultant ensures compliance with employment law and clarity for both parties.

Induction

It is good practice to offer a structured induction to new starters. Key points include:

- The induction might involve a formal welcome meeting, a guided tour of the premises, access to systems and equipment and a meeting with key team members.

- New staff members should be introduced to the organisation's vision, mission, values, history and strategic plan.

- New staff members should receive an induction pack containing the staff handbook, key policies (including safeguarding, health and safety, confidentiality and IT use) and practical information on how to claim expenses, report sickness or book annual leave.

Probationary period

Good supervision is especially important during the probationary period, when you and your new employee are getting to know each other and they are becoming familiar with the organisation. This stage is a time to assess whether the role is a good fit, which is why statutory notice periods for both employer and employee are usually much shorter than for established staff. The shortest recommended notice period to ensure you are complying with employment legislation is one week.

It is essential you use this time effectively and set out a training plan, with detailed milestones that should be achieved by the end of each review period. You should be able to clearly communicate expectations to the new member of staff and give them the opportunity and appropriate support to meet those expectations before the end of the probationary period. While we all want our new staff members to settle in well, some hires just don't work out, and it is important to assess early on whether someone is capable of undertaking the role they have been hired for. Retaining an ineffective team member can reduce morale on both sides and impact services.

Ongoing supervision

Ongoing supervision is essential. This doesn't mean constantly monitoring someone's work but instead giving them time to reflect, learn and feel supported. Regular one-to-one meetings should be scheduled to review progress and workload, celebrate successes, discuss concerns and agree on next steps. Good supervision is a two-way street, allowing both the staff member and their line manager to raise issues, learn together and agree on priorities.

Annual appraisals or performance reviews can be helpful in recognising progress, setting new goals and identifying training needs, but they should not replace regular conversations. Staff members should know where they stand and who they can approach for support or guidance at any time, and feel that their contribution is recognised throughout the year.

Creating a fair and inclusive workplace

As mentioned in Chapter 8, employers must comply with the equality legislation, including the Equality Act 2010, which protects people from discrimination on the basis of nine protected characteristics:

1. Age

2. Disability

3. Gender reassignment

4. Marriage and civil partnership

5. Pregnancy and maternity

6. Race

7. Religion or belief

8. Sex

9. Sexual orientation[33]

Inclusive practice means going beyond compliance and thinking about how recruitment, training, supervision and leadership create a sense of belonging. It means checking whether policies on flexible working, parental leave or reasonable adjustments are actually being used and understood. It's about considering how your organisation's culture – spoken or unspoken – supports or excludes different people.

Wellbeing

An emphasis on mental health and wellbeing in the workplace is becoming increasingly important. Not-for-profit organisations, and charities in particular, can be emotionally demanding workplaces, where staff work closely with service users, often dealing with crisis situations or juggling multiple roles.

Employers have a duty of care and should actively support staff wellbeing. This might include offering flexible working hours, encouraging breaks and rest, signposting for mental health support, or at least checking in regularly with all employees.

Addressing poor performance

Sometimes, even with the best supervision and a supportive environment, a staff member may not be meeting the standards expected of their role.

When considering the reasons for poor performance, it is useful to distinguish between capability and conduct.

Capability issues arise when someone lacks the necessary skills, knowledge or capacity to meet expectations, despite genuine effort. Conduct issues, by contrast, occur when an individual is unwilling to perform as required, and this is often linked to attitude, motivation or behaviour.

Conduct issues are usually dealt with under the disciplinary procedure. Where poor performance and poor conduct overlap, it may be appropriate to run a performance management process alongside disciplinary action, provided each process is kept clear and distinct to avoid confusion.

In the case of capability-related underperformance, the supervisor should initially meet with the individual to explain the concerns, listen to their perspective and agree on the desired outcomes. This discussion should be approached with empathy, avoiding assumptions about the reasons for underperformance. Factors that may contribute to difficulties include:

- Personal circumstances
- Lack of clarity in the role
- Insufficient training
- Unrealistic workload expectations

This discussion should be followed up with a performance improvement plan (PIP) – a formal document that sets out clear expectations, specific areas where performance is falling short, and the support that will be provided to help the individual improve. It is designed to give a fair and transparent framework for turning things around.

The plan itself should contain specific and measurable outcomes, set realistic timescales and include milestones for review, much like the structured induction plan for new starters. Support might involve additional training, arranging for the person to shadow a more experienced colleague, or adjusting workload priorities.

Regular supervision meetings during this period provide an essential opportunity to give constructive feedback, recognise progress and address any further barriers. Documentation is important, both to provide clarity for all involved and to protect the organisation in case the plan does not result in the desired improvement and further action becomes necessary.

If the individual meets the objectives, the PIP can be formally closed, with the staff member's achievement acknowledged and celebrated. If performance remains unsatisfactory, you will need to follow your organisation's disciplinary process, ensuring fairness and compliance with employment law.

Disciplinary procedures

You should have written disciplinary procedures to deal with employee performance and conduct and tell your staff what they are. This could be a section in the staff handbook or a standalone policy easily available to all. Your rules must state what behaviour is acceptable and unacceptable and the actions you can take if the rules are broken. Action can range from a verbal warning up to dismissal, depending on the behaviour, but it must be proportionate.

At its most basic, the government states that the disciplinary procedure should start with a letter to the employee clearly explaining the issue, which is followed up with an invitation to a meeting to discuss the problems.[34] Adequate time should be taken for consideration of the matter following the meeting, but the individual must be given the disciplinary decision in a timely manner and have a chance to appeal the decision.

The government strongly recommends that you follow the Acas Code of Practice for any discipline or grievance case.[35] If the case should reach an employment tribunal, the procedure followed by the employer will be scrutinised, and failure to follow a full and fair procedure could increase any tribunal award to the employee.

As employment law is continually updated, this is an area where I would strongly recommend taking professional advice, both in regularly reviewing your policies to ensure they meet current employment law standards and certainly before instigating a disciplinary process.

Key points

- **Becoming an employer.** It is essential to plan carefully before taking on paid employees, including around the role itself, budgeting for salary and employer costs, and tax and pension obligations.

- **Recruitment, induction and supervision.** You need to ensure that your recruitment processes are fair, transparent and inclusive, with clear job descriptions, structured shortlisting and interviews, and legally compliant contracts. New staff should receive a structured induction, probationary support, and regular and supportive ongoing supervision.

- **Ongoing management.** Poor performance should be addressed through supportive measures, including open discussions and PIPs.

- **Disciplinary procedures.** Poor conduct should be dealt with through the disciplinary procedure.

10

Supporting People And Managing Conflict

This chapter explores how to create an environment where staff and volunteers feel valued, safe and heard. Supporting people and responding with care when tensions arise is part of your responsibility as a leader.

Healthy organisations actively invest in people's well-being. They create structures for supervision, processes for raising concerns and policies for resolving disagreements, all in a respectful and constructive way.

There are differences in the terminology used in relation to staff and volunteers, to reflect and maintain the separate legal status of each category. I recap the differences in the table below.

Paid staff	Volunteers
Covered by employment law and statutory rights.	Not covered by employment law. Volunteers have no employee or worker rights.
Have a contract of employment and written terms.	Don't have a contract. Use a volunteer agreement or volunteer policy.
Formal supervision and monitoring against the job description and targets. Formal appraisal procedures.	Lighter-touch support and supervision to ensure they can perform the role safely and effectively.
Problems are dealt with under a formal disciplinary procedure in line with Acas guidance.	Issues are dealt with through a problem-solving process, not a disciplinary procedure.
Can face formal sanctions (verbal warning, written warning, dismissal).	No formal sanctions. Issues should be documented with a note of concern. If issues persist, the organisation may end the volunteering arrangement or ask the volunteer to step down.
Have the right to be accompanied at disciplinary hearings and to appeal decisions.	It's good practice to allow a volunteer to bring a friend or supporter to meetings, but they have no legal right to an appeal process.
Employers must keep detailed records for legal compliance.	Organisations should keep notes for consistency and fairness, but there is no statutory framework.

Supervision of staff

Effective supervision is based on trust. It should be confidential within agreed parameters (particularly where safeguarding is involved), focused and two-way. The team member should feel listened to and able to influence the agenda. Notes from supervision meetings should be documented and agreed by both parties. These notes can help track progress, identify recurring concerns and celebrate development.

Supervision should be a regular, one-to-one meeting with a manager or team leader. It could be monthly, bimonthly or quarterly, depending on the role. These conversations should be planned, protected and purposeful, with both parties given time to prepare, and the tone should be respectful, supportive and constructive.

A supervision session might explore:

- Workload priorities

- The balance between delivery and administration

- Training needs

- Experiences of partnership working

- Wellbeing

Support for volunteers

Support may be less formal but it is no less important. Many volunteers are highly committed but may lack clear role boundaries or feel unsure about how to raise issues.

Support might include:

- Assigning a named volunteer supervisor and offering regular check-ins

- Short conversations after each session to help volunteers feel connected, valued and confident

- Opportunities for volunteers to reflect together to foster community and prevent isolation

Identifying and addressing stress or burnout

While working or volunteering in the not-for-profit sector can be deeply fulfilling, it can also be emotionally and physically demanding, leading to stress or burnout.

Stress

Short-term stress is often situational, for example in response to a difficult conversation or a looming deadline. The symptoms may include restlessness, feelings of overwhelm, difficulty concentrating, disrupted sleep or emotional responses like frustration or anxiety. These moments can often be managed with timely support, which might include reassurance from a supervisor, a chance to talk things through, temporary work reassignment or a short break.

More concerning is longer-term, chronic stress. This is harder to spot and often presents as subtle changes in behaviour, for example a normally punctual person starting to miss deadlines or a volunteer suddenly seeming disengaged. Physical symptoms can include headaches, stomach problems or frequent colds. This is why policies like sickness absence monitoring and return-to-work interviews can be a powerful welfare management tool.

Burnout

Burnout is a state of emotional, physical and mental exhaustion caused by prolonged stress. Individuals may experience fatigue, irritability, reduced performance, withdrawal, cynicism or a sense of hopelessness. They may stop contributing, take unplanned absences or lose confidence in themselves or others. Burnout often follows a gradual buildup of low-level stress that has gone unrecognised or not been addressed.

Addressing stress and burnout

Employers have a legal duty to assess and manage work-related stress. Once an organisation reaches five or more employees, a written stress risk assessment is required under health and safety law.[36] Supervisors and managers should be trained to notice changes in behaviour and foster an environment where people feel safe to speak openly. Regular one-to-ones, staff surveys or wellbeing audits can help identify concerns before they become critical.

To reduce stress, it helps to encourage people to make space in the day to pause, move, eat or reflect, as well as reminding them to schedule their annual leave for proper breaks throughout the year. It's important to review workloads honestly with the team and look for pinch points. The not-for-profit sector has its own rhythms of work, often with peaks and troughs of activity throughout the year, and rescheduling or outsourcing some of the less urgent tasks could ease the pressure on staff and volunteers.

It also helps to normalise conversations about stress. Some organisations offer counselling, coaching or peer support groups, creating spaces where people can explore their stress without judgement. Even informal buddy systems can help, particularly in supporting people who are new or working in isolated roles. Those who feel part of a supportive team are more likely to stay resilient.

Another effective option is to offer an employee assistance programme (EAP) which can provide confidential services such as counselling, legal and financial advice to staff experiencing personal or professional challenges. These can be introduced quite cost effectively, even for small organisations.

Leaders play a crucial role here. If they model self-care, boundary setting and reflection, others will feel they have permission to do the same. Conversely, if leaders work through illness, answer emails at midnight or constantly talk about being overloaded, they may unintentionally signal that these are the expectations of the organisation.

Understanding conflict and how to address it

Conflict isn't always a sign that something has gone wrong; in fact, it can be a vital part of a healthy organisation. In not-for-profits, where people often bring with them strong values, lived experience and emotional investment, it is particularly important to create a culture where disagreement is handled in a safe and constructive manner.

Differences in working styles, communication, values or expectations can all lead to friction. Avoiding disagreement altogether can lead to resentment and stagnation, while unmanaged conflict can become personal, damaging or divisive.

Addressing conflict

People need to feel safe to raise concerns and confident that they will be taken seriously. Encouraging a culture where disagreement is welcomed, as long as it is respectful, can help prevent issues from becoming personal.

Workplace conflict, if handled well, can be a source of growth. If mishandled, it can damage trust, morale and retention. Having clear grievance and disciplinary procedures and using them fairly is essential, as is encouraging a culture where staff can speak up early and know they will be heard with respect. Managers should be supported with training in conflict resolution and communication skills. In many cases the first step is a facilitated conversation, led by a manager, a peer or an external facilitator. The aim is to create a safe space where each person can explain how they see the situation, how it has affected them and what they need to move forward. The focus is on building shared understanding, not taking sides or deciding which person is right or wrong.

Many issues can be prevented by:

- Setting out clear expectations through role descriptions, values statements and codes of conduct
- Training staff and volunteers in active listening, feedback skills and basic conflict resolution

If people know what respectful behaviour looks like, they're more likely to notice and challenge breaches.

Where informal approaches don't resolve the issue, or where serious concerns exist, you may need to move on to a formal process.

Grievance procedures, complaints, concerns and mediation

A note of caution first: this section is intended only to make you aware of your responsibilities, not to be a definitive guide. Procedures relating to the employment of staff are written into UK employment law, with specific processes that need to be followed and there are serious consequences for getting this wrong. As HR law is a complex subject and the legislation is updated regularly, please take independent advice before following any guidance in this book.

Grievance procedures

A grievance procedure is a formal policy that explains how staff (it only applies to employees) can raise concerns about unfair treatment, bullying, discrimination or other forms of conflict. It ensures there is a clear, consistent and fair process which protects the rights of everyone involved.

A typical grievance begins with a concern being raised, either verbally or in writing, to a named manager or board member. While many grievances are about relationships with managers or colleagues they can also relate to:

- Terms and conditions of employment

- Work environment

- Organisational changes

- Unfair treatment

- Management decisions

The organisation should confirm receipt and then investigate the concern thoroughly, including holding meetings with the parties involved, at which the individual may be accompanied by a colleague or representative. Once a decision has been reached, it should be shared clearly and respectfully, and the staff member should be informed of their right to appeal if they disagree with the decision.

Grievance policies must be accessible, regularly reviewed and in line with good practice, for example the Acas Code of Practice.[37] They should be included in staff handbooks and discussed as part of the induction and training process.

When a grievance isn't resolved

There are times when the outcome of a grievance procedure may not be satisfactory, either for the person who raised the issue or for the organisation.

If a grievance investigation reveals serious misconduct or ongoing poor behaviour from an individual member of staff, it may trigger a disciplinary process. This must follow a fair and structured procedure, aligned with the Acas Code of Practice, which includes a clear explanation of the issue, a formal meeting, the opportunity to respond and the right of appeal.

Outcomes could range from a formal warning to dismissal, depending on the severity of the issue and any previous incidents.

Problem-solving procedure

Volunteers are not covered by the same legal protections because grievances are an employment right. However, the NCVO strongly recommends organisations develop a *problem-solving procedure* to deal with complaints, problems, issues or concerns, either from or about the volunteer, which follows a similar, fair process, without suggesting or implying any contractual relationship.[38]

Volunteers might raise a concern about:

- The way they are treated

- Resources or safety

- Organisational decisions that affect their role

If a volunteer has raised a concern against a paid member of staff and it is upheld, this may trigger disciplinary procedures for the staff member. When a member of staff has raised a grievance which involves a volunteer (who doesn't have contractual rights), the approach should be proportionate. The available remedies will be included in the problem-solving procedure. Always aim for resolution and learning but recognise when it may no longer be appropriate for someone to continue in a role.

Ultimately, the goal is to protect the wellbeing of everyone involved and uphold the values of the organisation.

Mediation

Mediation can be another valuable tool for resolving conflict, particularly when the individuals will need to work together in the future, but both parties must be open to the process. A mediator is a neutral third party who facilitates a structured conversation, where those in conflict listen to each other, understand each other's views and explore a way forward.

Mediation can be used early as a preventative step, or after formal procedures to rebuild trust. It is confidential, voluntary and future-focused. Organisations can train staff or board members in mediation, or access external mediators through specialist services.

Key points

- **Supervision for staff.** Effective supervision, based on trust and confidentiality, must ensure the employee understands what is required of them, feels listened to and able to influence the agenda. Supervision can be through structured one-to-ones or regular check-ins, and they should help the individual feel valued, safe and connected.

- **Support for volunteers.** Volunteer support is less formal but based on the same principles. It could include having a named supervisor with whom the volunteer can discuss problems, short debriefs after each session, and opportunities to reflect with peers to encourage a sense of community and combat isolation.

- **Stress and burnout.** Leaders and supervisors should recognise signs of stress and burnout. This can be achieved by normalising open conversations about wellbeing and creating supportive processes such as workload reviews, breaks and peer support.

- **Managing conflict.** Conflict can have positive repercussions if handled well. Organisations should set clear expectations and train staff in communication and conflict resolution.

11

Working With Contractors

This chapter explores how to work effectively with contractors, whether for one-off projects, specialist services or flexible support. It guides you through the legal differences between employment and contracting, how to find the right people and how to set clear expectations. The chapter also covers managing relationships and ensuring quality, and what to do if problems arise.

The difference between an employee and a contractor

Employees are bound by their employment contract, and you can specify exactly when and where they work, what tasks they undertake and in which order they are completed. This can be preferable, for example, if you have a public-facing service and require someone to be in a specific place at a specific time.

Contractors are engaged under a commercial contract to deliver specific outcomes, but how they fulfil that contract is entirely at their discretion. They have the right to work when they choose, using the tools of their own choice. They also have the scope to choose how many staff will be supplied to undertake the contract, and they can replace or substitute those staff members at will. Contractors are responsible for their own tax affairs, so there are no employer on-costs for the organisation.

While genuine contractors do not accrue employment rights with your organisation, you need to be careful to confirm the deemed employment status of any individuals you engage, using HMRC's CEST (check employment status for tax) tool.[39] This was developed to protect individuals who were being wrongly classified as self-employed by companies who wanted to avoid providing employment benefits.

When to use a contractor

Contractors can bring a range of benefits in particular circumstances. For example, an organisation may need someone with a specific skillset for a short-term project. This could be a discrete implementation project, where a specialist is needed; or during a period of change within the organisation, such as contracting an interim CEO while the organisation hires a new, permanent member of staff.

Some organisations hire contractors to support specific parts of their services as an alternative to employing staff, eg membership services or marketing. This can have advantages because the employment responsibilities lie entirely with the contractor, meaning the organisation does not have to worry about providing equipment, keeping up to date with employment law regulations or handling day-to-day management of staff.

Finding and engaging the right contractor

The following three steps are vital when you are looking to start work with a new contractor:

1. Preparation

2. Selection

3. Contract

Preparation

Before you begin looking for a contractor, you should take the time to write a clear project brief, similar to the job description used in staff recruitment. This brief will outline:

- The background and purpose of the work

- The specific outcomes you want to achieve

- The scope, timescale and budget available

Selection

Contractors can be found through various chan-nels. Personal recommendations, professional net-works, directories and platforms like the NCVO, CharityComms or LinkedIn can help identify qualified providers to approach with your requirements. For larger projects, you may need to issue a public tender or invite multiple proposals.

Once you've shortlisted candidates, take time to assess them carefully. Ask for examples of similar work, speak to previous clients and explore whether the candidates understand the ethos and context of your organisation. Cultural fit can be just as important as technical skill. A contractor who is responsive and respectful and who understands the constraints of working within a not-for-profit organisation may be far more effective than one of the 'big name' consultancies.

Contract

When you've chosen a contractor, it's vital to formal-ise the relationship with a contract. This should set out what is expected of both the contractor and your organisation and what remedies are available if either of you breaks the agreement or if the contractor fails to deliver the required services. It should also include terms around:

- Confidentiality

- Ownership of work, for example, who owns a report or a website design

- Data protection

- What happens if the agreement is terminated early

Even if the project is relatively small, having a written contract helps prevent misunderstandings and protects both parties.

A service level agreement (SLA) is an extension of the contract and details exactly what will be delivered, how and when it will be delivered, and how much and when the contractor will be paid. It can go into far greater detail than the headline contract and can be amended (by agreement) as project needs change, without requiring a new contract.

While contracts can legally be formed by verbal agreement, if you are obtaining services on behalf of your organisation, it is best practice to ensure the terms are documented and signed by both parties.

Managing the contractor relationship

While contractors are expected to be self-sufficient in their work, a well-managed relationship is crucial for balancing autonomy with accountability.

Start with a welcome meeting or phone call, including the supervisor or team who will be working directly with the contractor. In many organisations those people won't have been involved in the engagement process, so this initial conversation is their chance to build rapport and establish mutual expectations. Go through the brief together, making sure everyone has the same understanding of timelines and deliverables. Confirm who the main point of contact will be on both sides and who else needs to be informed or consulted when decisions are required.

Provide relevant documents, context and points of contact. For example, if a contractor is designing your annual report, they'll need branding guidelines, last year's report and access to those overseeing the content. Making this easy shows respect for their time and sets them up for success.

Keep a written record of key agreements and decisions to help prevent misunderstandings, particularly if there are changes mid-project that affect the timeline or project scope.

Throughout the project, remain actively engaged. To keep the project on track, stay in touch, provide prompt feedback and respond to queries quickly. If a draft or deliverable isn't quite right, explain why. Good contractors value honest, constructive feedback because it helps them align their work to your needs.

What to do if things go wrong

Even with the best intentions and proper planning, things can sometimes go wrong. The work may not meet your standards, deadlines may slip, or communication can break down. Follow these five vital steps to help resolve any such situation:

1. Take action

2. Keep records

3. Check agreed terms

4. Communicate clearly and formally

5. Escalate if necessary

1. Take action

The first and most important step is to act early. If you sense something is not quite right, don't ignore the problem in the hope it will resolve itself. Delays in raising issues often make things worse.

Approach the contractor calmly and constructively. Ask how things are progressing, raise any concerns clearly, and offer to talk things through. Often, the root cause is something simple like miscommunication, a misunderstood brief or a personal issue.

2. Keep records

Document the concerns and any discussions you have and share your notes with the contractor. If the issue relates to the quality of work, be specific. Clarify exactly what's missing or unclear, ideally referring back to your original brief or any subsequent clarifications. For example, you might say, *We were expecting the report to include three case studies and evidence from our last campaign. Could we revisit that section?*

3. Check agreed terms

Sometimes it becomes clear that a contractor cannot or will not meet expectations. This might be due to capacity, skills or simply a poor fit with your organisation. In these cases, return to the contract or agreement. What does it say about delivery deadlines, payment milestones or termination clauses?

If the contract was well drafted, it should offer a framework for resolution, whether that is in withholding final payment, agreeing a revised schedule or ending the contract early.

4. Communicate clearly and formally

Always keep communication professional and focused on the issue. Be fair but firm. Acknowledge the contractor's efforts where possible, but be clear about what has gone wrong.

If you ultimately decide to terminate the contract, do so in writing, referencing the terms you're relying on. For example, *As per clause 4.3, we are ending the contract due to non-delivery of the final report by the agreed date.* Be sure to adhere to any notice periods or return of property clauses. Ending a contract without following due process can expose your organisation to unnecessary risk or reputational harm.

5. Escalate if necessary

In more serious situations, for example where there is a suspicion of misconduct, financial mismanagement or harm to beneficiaries, you may need to escalate the issue. That might include reporting concerns to your board, funders or insurers. In rare cases, legal advice may be required. This is particularly relevant if data protection, safeguarding or health and safety obligations have been breached.

After the situation is resolved, take time to reflect as a team. What warning signs were missed? Was the brief clear and realistic? Were there points where closer oversight could have helped? Learning from a difficult experience is just as valuable as celebrating a successful one.

It is also worth reviewing your procurement and contracting processes. Consider adding clearer milestones, building in a midpoint review or using a checklist to confirm mutual expectations. Over time, your organisation will build confidence in spotting early red flags and knowing when and how to intervene.

Key points

- **Benefits.** Contractors can provide essential services without the need to manage long-term employment responsibilities. You still need to be careful in preparation, selection, agreements, management and ongoing communication to ensure the work is completed by the right person and to your requirements.

- **Issues.** If things go wrong, you will need to address any issues promptly and professionally. After the issue has been resolved, it's important to reflect on the process to avoid recurrence of problems in future contractor relationships.

12

Communication, Collaboration And Culture

Communication, collaboration and culture are the glue that hold an organisation together. They influence morale, reputation and stakeholder engagement. In small or volunteer-led groups, these dynamics often emerge informally. In larger or more complex organisations, they may be supported by formal strategies and systems. In every case, they require care and attention.

This chapter explores how not-for-profits can communicate with purpose and clarity, both internally and externally, to build healthy, inclusive cultures and create environments where collaboration thrives.

Communication

Communication takes on various forms in any organisation. Here we'll consider the differences between communication within your organisation and communication with external stakeholders, and the importance of accessibility for all concerned.

Internal communication and meetings

Strong internal communication ensures that everyone in your organisation feels informed, involved and valued. Whether your team is made up of volunteers, paid staff, contractors or a mixture of all three, everyone needs to understand what is happening, why it matters and how they can contribute.

Communication within a not-for-profit will take many forms – electronic and face-to-face, formal and informal. There is no one-size-fits-all solution. What works for a small local project, for example, will likely not suit a growing regional organisation. Consistency, clarity and accessibility in communication are key. Messages should be easy to understand, timely and tailored to the audience. If someone needs to act on information they receive, they should know exactly what they need to do and by when.

Having a clear line-management structure can help, with individuals given a designated point of contact for problems and concerns. This consistency helps facilitate a trusted relationship and ensures targeted delivery of relevant messages and information.

Regular meetings – weekly check-ins, monthly all-team sessions or quarterly board reviews, to name just a few – offer opportunities to share updates, build relationships and address challenges. Hybrid, remote and flexible working can present a particular challenge in regard to meetings, and it's important to use inclusive practices to give everyone a chance to be heard. You should circulate an agenda in advance of any meeting to allow individuals to prepare effectively or contribute if they cannot attend, and then ensure documents and decisions are shared after the meeting. You can also consider offering information in multiple formats, using plain English.

Active listening is crucial, and good communicators create opportunities for others to speak and feel heard. Creating mechanisms for anonymous feedback or small-group discussions can help draw out quieter voices and ensure more equitable participation.

As organisations grow, a communications protocol can help by setting out who needs to know what, when they need it and through which channels. For example, you might decide that urgent updates are sent via text message, strategic information is discussed in team meetings and policy changes are emailed with clear summaries and links to the full documents.

A communications protocol also helps avoid overload and duplication of information and siloed working.

External communication and community engagement

Your organisation's reputation depends not only on what you do but also on how well you explain it. Good external communication tells your story and builds trust with funders, service users, supporters and the wider public.

At its most basic, this includes publishing up-to-date contact details, a welcoming website and a clear description of your work. As you grow, you might add newsletters, social media updates, media coverage and details of outreach events. No matter the size of the organisation, the same principles apply:

- Know your audience

- Speak with purpose

- Keep your message consistent

A communication strategy doesn't have to be complex; it simply clarifies who you want to reach, what you want to say and how you will say it. It might prioritise building relationships with local councillors, raising awareness among your target audience or sharing case studies with funders. It might set out guidelines for tone of voice and branding or for how staff and volunteers can talk about your work.

Here are some final key points to note when you are looking to improve your external communication methods:

- Marketing is about broadcasting a message. Engagement is about creating a dialogue.

- Community consultation, service user feedback sessions, suggestion boxes and listening exercises can all gather information that can be used to strengthen your work.

- When service users or members are invited to help shape programmes, policies or messaging, their lived experience brings insights you might otherwise miss.

Information accessibility

Accessibility, ensuring that everyone can access and understand what you are saying, is a key part of communication. Here are some key points to remember when creating any internal or external communications:

- Make sure your printed marketing material is easy to read and is written in plain English.

- Consider translating your material into the languages used within your community.

- Think about the needs of those with disabilities, including providing access to the information in large print or braille or providing the information in video format.

It's also important to check your digital communications meet accessibility standards. Under the Equality Act 2010[40] (for England, Wales and Scotland) and the Disability Discrimination Act 1995[41] (for Northern Ireland), organisations have a duty to make reasonable adjustments to ensure disabled people are not disadvantaged. While we may be familiar with this applying to physical access, employment and service delivery, reasonable adjustments must also be made for digital content, websites and apps.

Public sector organisations are bound by the Web Content Accessibility Guidelines (WCAG),[42] which were developed by the World Wide Web Consortium to support The Public Sector Bodies (Websites and Mobile Applications) Accessibility Regulations 2018.[43]

Under WCAG principles, digital information should be perceivable, operable, understandable and robust, often represented by the acronym POUR. While the legislation does not apply to not-for-profit or private organisations, following the WCAG POUR principles is considered best practice and demonstrates reasonable adjustment.

Collaboration

Collaboration is the process of working together with others towards a shared goal, pooling knowledge, skills and resources to achieve outcomes that would be harder to reach alone.

Good collaboration requires knowing when to lead and when to step back, when to compromise and when to challenge. Organisations that collaborate well tend to be more creative and solve problems more effectively and are often able to achieve more with fewer resources. Collaboration also builds resilience, as networks of partners can offer mutual support and shared learning, making the organisation more adaptable to change.

Culture

Culture is the shared set of values, norms and behaviours that determine how people experience your organisation. It influences how people treat each other, how decisions are made and how conflict is handled. A positive culture supports psychological safety and encourages people to speak up, ask questions and admit mistakes without fear of punishment or exclusion, thereby encouraging curiosity, openness and shared learning. A positive, open organisational culture makes collaboration with others more effective because people feel safe to share ideas, admit mistakes and listen to different perspectives without fear of criticism.

The role of shared values

Culture, at its core, is rooted in values – the deeply held principles that shape what we prioritise, how we treat others and how we want our organisation to be. In not-for-profit organisations, shared values are often stated within vision and mission statements, strategic plans or team charters.

Culture is shaped by leadership but built by everyone. When leaders model respect, transparency and reflection, others are more likely to do the same. Culture is reinforced in day-to-day actions – how information is shared, how feedback is given, what behaviour is challenged and what is ignored. When leaders consistently model the organisation's values in how they communicate, the way they make decisions and the way they respond to challenge, it creates a ripple effect throughout the team.

Leaders who admit mistakes, invite feedback and make space for others to shine demonstrate humility and a growth mindset. For example, if one of your organisation's stated values is equity, then modelling might involve actively rotating speaking opportunities in meetings, offering flexible volunteering options or reviewing policies with a lens on inclusion. If learning is a core value, it might show up in how leaders respond to failure, encouraging reflective practice and treating mistakes as learning moments rather than personal failures.

The clearer and more consistent your organisation's values are, the easier it is for everyone to understand what is expected of them. This is particularly important during growth, crisis or transition, when uncertainty can challenge even the most cohesive teams.

Values must be congruent with the organisation's goals and revisited regularly. Hosting values workshops and embedding values into recruitment, induction and performance conversations all help ensure they remain meaningful and relevant.

Key points

- **Communication.** Strong internal communication, including regular meetings, ensures that everyone feels informed, valued and listened to. Good external communication builds trust and engagement with stakeholders. Accessibility across all forms of communication is vital.

- **Culture and collaboration.** An open and positive culture, modelled by the organisation's leaders, supports psychological safety and encourages people to speak up, ask questions and admit mistakes, leading to a happier and more productive environment. It also increases trust, leading to improved internal and external collaboration.

PART THREE
DAY-TO-DAY OPERATIONS

In Part Three we focus on the practical side of operations: delivering services, engaging members and supporters, running events, managing partnerships, raising funds and securing grants. These are the activities that keep your organisation active, visible and financially sustainable.

We begin with membership and service delivery, as many not-for-profits exist to provide some form of benefit or support to their members or wider community. Whether you run a community group, a professional association or a service charity, this chapter will help you understand who your audience is, how to design and deliver effective services and how to build meaningful membership models that encourage ongoing engagement and loyalty.

Next we turn to event planning and execution. Events can be a brilliant way to raise funds, build relationships and showcase your work, but they require careful planning. Chapter 14 takes you through that process, from deciding what kind of event is right to planning the details, promoting the event and ensuring things go smoothly on and after the day.

Then we explore partnerships and working across sectors. Collaboration can open up new opportunities and increase your organisation's reach and impact, particularly when you are working alongside others who share your goals. This might include other charities, community groups, public bodies and businesses. We'll look at informal collaborations and strategic alliances, as well as the benefits and challenges of cross-sector working.

Chapter 16 introduces advocacy and campaigning. Not every not-for-profit is involved in this area, but for many it's a central part of their mission. Whether you're trying to change a policy, influence decision makers or raise awareness, you'll learn about how to design campaigns, choose tactics and channels, and stay within the law while making your voice heard.

We then turn to the essential topic of grants and funding. Many organisations rely on grants to fund their services, projects or core costs. Chapter 17 breaks down the different types of funders and what they're looking for in an application. You'll find guidance on writing clear, compelling bids, managing restricted and unrestricted funds, and meeting funder expectations.

Finally, we address fundraising more broadly. Beyond grants, there are many ways to raise money, from collecting tins and charity raffles to direct debits, legacy giving and online appeals. Chapter 18 covers the legal frameworks you need to be aware of, introduces the key fundraising regulators and provides practical advice to help you fundraise legally, ethically and effectively.

13

Service Delivery And Membership Models

What does good service delivery look like? Whether you offer services to the general public or operate as a membership organisation, being clear about who you serve and how you do that work is vital to delivering high-quality, inclusive, mission-driven work. This chapter helps you understand your audience, design services that meet real needs and manage delivery in a sustainable and responsive way.

Membership is central to the identity and sustainability of some groups, for example professional membership associations like the General Medical Council or the Institute of Chartered Accountants in England and Wales. For others, such as Cancer Research UK or the

RNLI, the focus is on delivering services funded by grants, contracts or donations. In both cases the principles of planning services are the same.

Understanding your audience

The first step in effective service delivery is understanding who you serve. This may sound obvious, but it is surprisingly common for organisations to make assumptions. Creating a clear picture of your intended users' needs, preferences, barriers and aspirations will help to ensure that your services are relevant and well used. For example, you might define your users as one of the following:

- Children and families in a particular neighbourhood

- People with lived experience of homelessness

- Older residents in a rural area

- People working in a specific profession or industry

The clearer your definition of your users, the better you can design your services to meet their needs. Particularly when working with the general public, you should consider factors most relevant to your intended users such as age, ethnicity, income level, language, digital access, education level, disabilities and long-term health conditions. These characteristics can significantly influence how people experience and engage with your services.

Formal research, surveys and community engagement exercises are good ways to begin to understand your users. Having board members and staff with lived experience can also be a great help here, both with interpreting the quantitative data and adding qualitative insights. Analysing usage data, attendance rates and feedback trends for services you already deliver can help identify gaps in reach or engagement.

Planning and delivering services

Service delivery is where you turn ideas and resources into activities, support and opportunities that improve people's lives. Planning service delivery involves thinking about what you will deliver and why, and to whom, where, when and how you deliver that service.

You should first consider the needs and priorities of your users and the outcomes you want to achieve. Then you can look at the resources – money, staff, space, etc – you have available to determine the optimal format for delivery, for example online or in person, one to one or in groups, at drop-in or scheduled appointments.

Service plans

A good service plan balances ambition with practicality, by:

- Setting out what you hope to deliver

- Including a delivery schedule, a budget and a monitoring framework

- Outlining who is responsible for each part of the service

- Identifying the potential risks and mitigations you will need to put in place

I have included an example service plan in the table below.

Section	Details to include
1. Purpose and context	What problem are you addressing?
	How does this fit your mission?
	Include background evidence or user consultation.
2. Intended users	Who are your target users?
	Describe their age, location, demographics, needs.
	Include how your service users were identified.
3. What you will deliver	What exactly will users receive or experience?
	Detail the activities, sessions, support, resources.

Section	Details to include
4. Intended outcomes	What difference will the service make in people's lives?
	Think about changes in confidence, wellbeing, access, knowledge, etc.
5. Location and timing	Where and when will your service be delivered?
	List delivery location(s), opening times, frequency.
	Is the service time limited or ongoing?
6. Method of delivery	How will your service be delivered?
	Describe delivery style and format, including who will deliver it and how users will access the service?
	Specify referral routes, booking systems, drop-in options, etc.
7. Resources required	What staffing, volunteers, money, space, equipment or IT are needed?
	Add estimated costs if you can.
8. Risks and mitigations	What might go wrong?
	Consider low attendance, safeguarding, funding, etc.
	How will you reduce those risks?
9. Roles and responsibilities	Who is responsible for each part of the service?
	List all roles, from planning to delivery to monitoring.
10. Monitoring and evaluation	How will you measure success?
	What will you monitor, when, and how?
	Who will do it?

Section	Details to include
11. Review and adaptation	When will the service be reviewed? Who is involved? What will trigger changes?

Delivery should be responsive and person-centred, which means listening and adapting as required. It may involve trial periods, pilot projects and phased rollouts. Designing services with users or creating user advisory panels can deepen insight and build trust.

Robust safeguarding procedures are critical. Organisations that support children or vulnerable adults need appropriate safeguarding policies, and you must ensure DBS checks are in place where required and offer regular safeguarding training. It is also important to have policies for health and safety, lone working, confidentiality and data protection, plus any other policies specific to your area of service.

Membership models and engagement

Membership organisations have an additional layer of audience definition. A member is someone who formally joins the organisation and who usually receives benefits, such as voting rights, newsletters or access to training, in return for an annual subscription fee.

Membership

If your organisation has members, it's important to be clear about who qualifies to become a member, how they join and what their rights and responsibilities are. This information should be easily accessible and reviewed regularly. A good membership model is clear about its audience, purpose and benefits. It should also clearly state any membership criteria or entrance requirements.

Memberships can be structured in a number of different ways. You may have individual membership or organisational membership (where groups or institutions are the members). You may even have different levels of membership, which offer enhanced benefits, either for an increased price or after obtaining specified qualifications or experience.

Your governing document or constitution should set out the rights and responsibilities of members. This includes how members are admitted and removed, voting rights, and any obligations such as paying a fee or attending meetings.

You'll also need a system for managing your membership. At the most basic level, you need to record member names, contact details, renewal dates and payment records. Very small organisations can use spreadsheets, while larger organisations will need to use a database. Many organisations will use dedicated

CRM (customer relationship management) software to automate communications, track engagement and analyse trends.

Engagement

Membership engagement is about the ongoing relationship and influences how members interact with and feel connected to your organisation. Engagement is vital for the ongoing success and growth of a membership organisation. Your organisation may have hundreds of members paying annual subscriptions, but if only a handful are regularly opening your emails, attending events or responding to surveys, it suggests low engagement. This can be a particular problem for professional organisations, where membership 'looks good on a CV'.

Engaged members are more likely to become an ambassador, volunteer or future board member. They are the ones who advocate for your organisation, increase your reach by recommending you to others and maintain your vital network and community.

Engagement is built through:

- Meaningful communication

- Involvement in decision making

- Volunteering opportunities

- Social events

- Shared goals

- Recognition

Membership benefits are often used as incentives to encourage people to join and renew their membership. They can include things like access to services, discounts on training, regular newsletters, exclusive events, or opportunities to influence the direction of the organisation.

Key points

- **Identifying your service users.** Understanding your audience is fundamental to the design, rollout and continued success of any service you deliver.

- **Planning and delivering your service delivery.** A service plan, including clear goals, delivery schedule, budget, monitoring framework, roles and responsibilities, and risks and mitigations is vital to successful service delivery.

- **Managing membership models.** With membership organisations, careful management is key, including details of your audience, current members and the purpose and benefits of membership. Maintaining membership engagement is core to ongoing success and growth.

14

Event Planning
And Execution

Events are a powerful way to raise awareness, build community and generate income. This chapter walks you through each stage of successful event management, from setting objectives and organising logistics to promotion and delivery. We'll also cover how to evaluate an event and follow up effectively.

Planning the right event

For an event to be successful it needs to be relevant, worthwhile and affordable for your target audience. The more clarity you have on the purpose of an event and the benefits of attendance, the easier it will be for you to plan the right format, reach the right audience and measure the outcomes.

I have given some examples of potential types of events to suit the purpose and audience in the table below.

Purpose of the event	Benefits of attendance	Ideal audience	Potential event types
Networking	Building new connections, sharing ideas, identifying collaboration opportunities	Sector professionals, local stakeholders, partners, funders	Meet-and-greet sessions, partnership breakfasts, networking evenings, peer learning circles
Learning or training	Gaining new skills, boosting confidence, improving effectiveness in role	Volunteers, staff, community members, service users	Workshops, training days, skill-building sessions, webinars
Celebration and recognition	Feeling valued, strengthening sense of belonging, reinforcing positive culture	Volunteers, donors, community beneficiaries, staff	Award ceremonies, anniversary events, appreciation lunches, milestone celebrations
Fundraising	Supporting a cause, enjoying an engaging social experience, seeing impact firsthand	Supporters, donors, local community, businesses	Gala dinners, fun runs, charity auctions, coffee mornings, community quizzes

Purpose of the event	Benefits of attendance	Ideal audience	Potential event types
Awareness raising and campaigning	Learning about key issues, connecting to a cause, taking action	General public, media, policymakers, service users	Public rallies, campaign launches, information stalls, themed awareness days
Consultation and feedback	Shaping services, sharing lived experience, feeling heard and involved	Service users, members, community groups, partners	Focus groups, survey feedback events, Q&A sessions
Recruitment	Discovering opportunities, asking questions, assessing good fit	Potential volunteers, trustees, staff and service users	Open days, information sessions, volunteer fairs, taster events
Income generation	Enjoying high-quality experiences while supporting a cause	Members, paying public, local businesses, wider community	Ticketed talks, training courses, exhibitions, workshops, seasonal markets
Service delivery and programme activities	Taking part in valued services, connecting with others, improving wellbeing	Beneficiaries, community groups, families	Drop-in sessions, themed activity days, outreach events, weekly clubs or classes

Purpose of the event	Benefits of attendance	Ideal audience	Potential event types
Strategic or internal planning	Contributing to future direction, feeling ownership, building trust internally	Staff, trustees, key volunteers, advisers	Away days, strategic planning workshops, governance review sessions

Detailed planning

Once you have your budget and capacity (see Chapter 21 for more information), there are some key considerations to be made:

- Venue and date

- Accessibility

- Planning schedule

- Risk assessments

- Other planning points

Venue and date

The type of event and the intended audience will determine the best type of venue and suitable days of the week, times of day, and whether to avoid or embrace school breaks and bank holidays. For example, the venue and date for a formal educational conference for adults will be different from those for a sports club festival aimed at children.

Accessibility

Choose a location that is easily accessible for the majority of your audience, and make sure you or a trusted colleague have visited it to confirm suitability. For example, it might be in a city centre with good transport links, or out of town with great parking. Consider accommodation requirements if the event extends into the evening or is held over multiple days.

Think about:

- Physical access, eg step-free venues, hearing loops, accessible toilets
- Communication access, eg plain English, translation, BSL interpretation
- Cultural access, eg dietary needs, prayer space, gender neutral toilets

If you're running an online or hybrid event, take into account digital accessibility like captioning, font size and audio quality. Remember the need for breaks, and offer ways for people to ask questions or participate that don't require speaking in front of a group. Creating a safe space policy or code of conduct helps set the tone.

Planning schedule

Large events on 'peak' dates could require planning as much as twelve to eighteen months in advance, whereas smaller midweek events may only require two or three months of planning.

Risk assessments

All events, even small and informal ones, should have a written risk assessment. This document needs to identify potential hazards, estimate the likelihood and impact of those hazards and detail the recommended actions in case those hazards materialise. I have provided an example risk assessment below.

Other planning points

Good communication with the venue is a vital part of the planning process. It is your responsibility to tell the venue how you want rooms set out, when and where you want the catering set up, what time your delegates are arriving and if there are any special access or dietary requirements.

At the first planning meeting with the venue you will need to agree on contract terms. Make a note of the minimum time ahead of the event it is possible to alter the booking, for example reducing or increasing numbers, and whether there are any penalties involved,

Hazard	Who might be harmed	Risk description	Current controls in place	Risk level (low/med/ high)	Additional actions needed	Person responsible	Deadline
Slips or trips due to wet floors	Attendees, volunteers	Someone could fall and be injured during the event.	Venue staff monitor and clean. Signs in use.	Medium	Check venue walkways in advance. Bring spare signage.	Event coordinator	Date of event
Allergic reaction to food (eg nuts, dairy, gluten)	Attendees with allergies	Someone may have a serious allergic reaction if food contains undeclared allergens.	Allergen information displayed clearly. Volunteers briefed. Prepackaged food with ingredient labels.	High	Check food supplier labelling. Display clear allergen signs. Provide allergen-free options. Ask attendees to flag allergies in advance.	Catering lead and event organiser	Date of event

which would have an impact on your event budget and your contingency provision. Most venues will let you reduce numbers before a certain date. Whether you can increase numbers will be dictated by the venue capacity and other bookings on site.

Events must be covered by a public liability policy. A venue may have its own policy that will cover your event, or you can purchase a standalone policy.

You also need to think ahead about:

- Safeguarding responsibilities

- Insurance

- Licences (if alcohol, live music or road closures are involved)

- Contact with local authorities and emergency services

Event promotion

As soon as you have decided on the date and venue, you should begin to market the event. Here are some key points to note:

- **Awareness.** Start raising awareness within your audience and get them to save the date or register an interest.

- **Ticket sales.** Decide whether you will sell tickets through your own website or premises, or via a third-party ticketing app. Don't forget to include booking fees or administration time in your budget calculations. Build the sales funnels and marketing assets early so they are ready ahead of the launch date.

- **Early-bird offers.** You might want to consider special offers for early registration to encourage ticket sales, the income from which you can use to pay deposits or fund other prepayments.

- **Special requirements.** You should collect details of dietary and accessibility requirements through your ticketing process. This information needs to be shared with the venue and caterer but is considered to be special category personal information under GDPR so it must be protected and limited to those who need to know.

- **Photography.** If you plan to capture photographs or video during the event, you must obtain consent. For adult-only events, it is enough to inform attendees that photographs will be taken and you will assume consent unless they specifically opt out. If children are present, whether the photographs are taken by a professional or by parents and carers, there must be individual photography consent in place and a register of anyone taking photographs so that images can be traced back to the source if required.

Final stages and hosting the event

It is good practice to have reached your breakeven ticket sales before your venue locks in minimum numbers. Depending on historical ticket sales and your audience, you can then make a best estimate of whether you are likely to make more sales closer to the event or whether you need to look at reducing numbers.

Slow sales could be a reflection of poor advertising or a lack of clear articulation of the benefits of attendance, so don't jump straight to reducing ticket prices. However, you should be prepared to cancel an event if you could lose more money than the deposit by running it for a small number of people.

You should schedule a final planning meeting with the venue two to four weeks ahead of the event. Share the final timings and confirm exactly how you want the space laid out and what level of service you expect on the day. Ask to meet your 'on the day' contact so that they recognise you and vice versa. This will make it much easier when you need to make last-minute changes on the day, which is inevitable, however well you plan ahead. Speakers don't always run to time, so you may have to flex the catering breaks. You may have guests not turn up or attendees arrive who haven't booked. Someone will inevitably have dietary requirements they failed to inform you of, and so forth. It's all part of the fun!

The day before the event, test your online platform or do a final walkthrough of the venue. Check signage, accessibility routes and facilities. Print out a run sheet with a minute-by-minute schedule of who is doing what and when. Have printed copies of the attendee list, floor plan, risk assessment, contact numbers and emergency plans available.

Finally, to avoid mixed messages, give one person overall responsibility for coordinating the event and acting as point of contact for attendees, speakers, the board and the venue.

Reflection

Following an event it is vital that, as part of your continual improvement process, you analyse and document what went well and what could be done better next time:

- **Finances.** Review your budget and timeline. Were your costs accurate, and did you sell as many tickets as you expected? Did you start planning early enough and was your marketing programme effective?
- **Feedback.** You should always request feedback from the attendees, speakers and guests, using simple surveys and informal conversations. Ask questions about their perception of the value of the event and any specific areas they particularly liked or felt could be improved on.

- **Evaluation.** It is also good practice to share feedback with the venue. Make a conscious effort to praise any members of staff who were particularly helpful and mention anything you particularly liked. Things do go wrong, but reflect on whether the issue was rectified to your satisfaction at the time.

- **Issues.** Sometimes issues couldn't be solved or weren't dealt with properly. If you need to give negative feedback, keep it dispassionate and factual. Remain kind and assume that everyone wanted to do a good job but that some things didn't quite meet the mark. If you are planning to use the venue again, tell them what you want to see next time in terms of planning or action. Often you will be offered preferential rates on your next booking or 'free' items of catering in compensation, which can equate to better value than receiving money off this year's final bill.

Key points

- **Planning.** First considerations for a successful event revolve around purpose, audience, format and venue. Special attention is needed regarding accessibility, risk assessments and insurance.

- **Promotion.** It's important to focus early on marketing and ticket sales, with initial income helping towards the venue deposit and other early costs.

- **Delivery and reflection.** Last-minute planning is vital, and it helps to appoint a single point of contact at your organisation to oversee the event on the day. After the event, evaluation of the event, together with feedback from attendees, will help towards the success of future events.

15

Partnerships And Working Across Sectors

Working in partnership can help your organisation achieve more, reach new audiences and share resources. This chapter looks at how to build and manage collaborations across the voluntary, public and private sectors. You'll learn about different types of partnership, from informal networks to formal alliances, and how to navigate the practicalities of joint working. We'll explore the benefits and risks as well as how to maintain alignment around shared goals.

National funders such as the National Lottery Community Fund or the UK Shared Prosperity Fund increasingly favour projects that demonstrate collaboration, recognising that systemic issues require joined-up responses.

Types of partnerships

Partnerships in the not-for-profit world take many different forms, from friendly, informal collaborations to highly structured, formal agreements. Some partnerships emerge organically and are built on local relationships and shared values. Others are strategic and contractual, driven by funding requirements or strategic delivery ambitions. Here you'll find an overview of the three main types of partnerships available to UK charities:

1. Informal collaborations

2. Formal partnerships

3. Strategic alliances

Informal collaborations

Informal collaborations often arise organically from relationships between individuals or organisations who identify common values or goals and see a chance to strengthen each other's work by sharing resources, skills and networks. They may start by signposting people between services, co-hosting events, sharing venues or jointly promoting campaigns.

One of the main benefits of informal collaborations is their flexibility and low risk. They can adapt quickly to changing needs, new opportunities and emerging crises. During the Covid pandemic, countless informal networks sprang up across the UK such as mutual-aid groups, food projects, churches and grassroots organisations, which coordinated responses in real time. These collaborations were often rapid, localised and highly responsive to community needs – something that would have been harder to achieve through formal contracting arrangements.

Because they are less constrained by legal agreements or fixed outputs, informal collaborations lend themselves to innovation. Partners can experiment and learn together, which makes these collaborations particularly well suited to early-stage initiatives or for small organisations testing new ideas before scaling. However, without formal documentation, it can be easy for misunderstandings to occur. Equally, as informal collaborations are based on personal relationships, they can be vulnerable to disruption when staff or volunteers move on.

Formal partnerships

Formal partnerships are the next step in a collaborative working arrangement and are underpinned by a legal agreement, often called a memorandum of understanding (MOU) or collaboration agreement. Crucially, each party remains legally separate while operating under the joint framework. This shouldn't be confused with a business partnership, as defined in the Partnership

Act 1890, which confers joint and several liability on the parties.[44]

The MOU will document:

- The purpose of the partnership
- The roles and responsibilities of each party
- The expected duration and outcomes

If you need a data sharing agreement, it must be compliant with UK GDPR, and there also needs to be a financial plan detailing who provides what resources and how to deal with a potential clawback of grant funding. The agreement should specify the governance structure, eg a joint steering committee or a single lead organisation, and the process for monitoring, review and evaluation.

Before entering into a formal partnership, it is important to do your due diligence. Make sure your prospective partner is solvent, legally compliant and shares your values. You also need to consider the potential risks of working with another organisation, particularly if you will be applying for shared funding or using data sharing agreements, and look to mitigate those risks.

Strategic alliances

Strategic alliances tend to involve a longer-term, more embedded relationship where two or more organisations align at a strategic level. This might involve shared service development, integration of administrative functions, shared staffing or a joint bid for funding. Strategic alliances are often formed to achieve significant joint outcomes such as delivering a major public service contract, running a multiyear programme or influencing mainstream policy.

Strategic alliances require significant investment in governance and relationship management. Partners must be prepared to participate in regular steering group meetings and shared reporting processes as well as agreeing in advance how risks – whether financial, legal or reputational – will be managed. The agreement could be an MOU, a contract or a joint venture agreement, and it must outline:

- Objectives

- Decision-making structures

- Funding arrangements

- Data sharing protocols

- Safeguarding

- Intellectual property rights

- Dispute resolution processes

It must also contain exit clauses to allow the alliance to be ended or renegotiated if circumstances change.

By working together over the long term, partners can scale their impact and enhance the credibility and leverage of each organisation. Funders and commissioners are often more likely to support collaborative bids from organisations that have a track record of working together.

However, in some cases alliances may create joint liabilities, or concerns can be raised about anti-competitive practices. Organisations should always seek legal advice before entering into agreements that involve shared financial risk, joint employment of staff or ownership of intellectual property.

Building strong partnerships

Strong partnerships are built on trust, mutual benefit and open and honest communication. The most successful partnerships are those where both sides are genuinely committed to the shared goal and where they have a sense of joint ownership and accountability.

It is important to invest time in getting to know your potential partner. Begin with informal conversations to explore their motivations and challenges and where your missions overlap. At the same time, be honest about your own capacity, strengths and needs.

One of the most important foundations of a strong partnership is alignment of values. This doesn't mean your organisations need to be identical in mission or methods, but you do need to be compatible in how you work and what you prioritise. If your values don't align, tension and frustration can ensue. Similarly, differing stances on equality, environmental practices or financial transparency can create conflict and reputational risk.

It is worth noting that alignment does not mean you have to be the same. Diverse perspectives can lead to innovation, as long as your core principles are respected.

Even when relationships are informal, it is vital to clarify expectations about who is doing what, when and why, but balancing formality with flexibility is a classic struggle. Too formal a partnership risks bureaucracy, delay and disengagement, while a too informal partnership may leave an organisation unprotected if things go wrong.

When there is more at stake such as shared data, responsibility for contracted services or working with vulnerable groups, more formal contracts and partnership agreements are appropriate.

Cross-sector working

Cross-sector working is a term that signifies organisations from different sectors or specialisms coming together to achieve something they couldn't do alone.

Public private partnerships (PPPs)

These are collaborations between government bodies and private businesses. In a traditional PPP, a private company might build and operate a piece of public infrastructure such as a school or hospital. While this model is most often discussed in terms of large-scale building projects, a growing number of local authorities and NHS trusts are now partnering with community organisations and social enterprises to deliver services that respond to local needs in a more tailored, community-centred way.

Voluntary sector state partnerships

These are arrangements between government and third-sector organisations (charities, CICs or social enterprises). The relationships can take many forms, from grant funding or service commissioning to policy work and delivery models.

Voluntary sector state partnerships have become increasingly vital as local authorities face funding cuts and turn to the voluntary sector for innovation, reach and trust in communities. However, these partnerships also raise questions around sustainability and independence when charities become closely tied to public service delivery.

Interdisciplinary or cross-thematic partnerships

These are collaborations between organisations tackling different aspects of need, for example a homelessness charity working with a mental health organisation, or a youth arts project linking with local police to address knife crime.

Cross-thematic in this sense means across fields of work rather than types of organisation. These are particularly effective when dealing with complex, interlinked social issues such as those where housing, health, employment, education and justice are all interconnected.

Key points

- **Benefits.** Strong partnerships add value to not-for-profits in a number of ways, including shared resources, skills and networks.

- **Types.** Choosing the ideal partnership depends on a range of factors, including the size and goals of your organisation and the level of flexibility you need. Types include informal collaborations, formal partnerships and strategic alliances as well as different options in cross-sector working.

- **Risks.** However formal or informal your partnership, due diligence, agreements and risk mitigation are vital to avoid misunderstandings and financial, legal or reputational risks.

16

Advocacy And Campaigning

Advocacy and campaigning can be powerful tools for change. While service delivery addresses immediate needs, advocacy and campaigning seek to change the root causes of injustice, inequality and exclusion.

Advocacy gives a voice to people and communities whose experiences might otherwise be ignored and helps bring about systemic change through influencing public attitudes, policy and practice.

Campaigning can take many forms, from petitions and protest to policy briefings and social media movements. What matters are clarity, credibility and a commitment to impact.

This chapter explores how to develop and deliver campaigns that are ethical, strategic and effective. It looks at how to plan your message, engage supporters, influence decision makers and manage risks, while staying true to your mission and values.

Advocacy and influence

Advocacy is the act of speaking or acting on behalf of others to bring about change. For some organisations this means supporting individuals to access their rights, for example by challenging a benefits decision or securing appropriate housing. This kind of individual advocacy focuses on case-by-case support.

Other organisations engage in collective advocacy, working with groups of people affected by an issue and raising shared concerns. An example could be a forum of disabled people lobbying for better public transport, or a network of those with lived experience of mental distress shaping policy around mental health provision.

There is also policy advocacy, which involves working behind the scenes to influence laws, strategies and funding priorities. This might include submitting consultation responses, briefing MPs or contributing to sector research.

Campaigning for action

Campaigning is about mobilisation. Campaigns are designed to raise public awareness and mobilise support to pressure decision makers to act in helping to address a particular issue. There is usually a specific call to action in the message. For example, not-for-profit organisations may ask supporters to use a social media hashtag, email their local MP or join a rally or campaign event.

Campaigning can include anything from media interviews and art installations to community marches or social media activism.

Designing a campaign

Every effective campaign begins with clarity about what you want to change and who has the power to change it. This focus helps avoid spreading your resources too thinly or falling into the trap of awareness raising with no clear objective.

It is important to start by researching any particular issue in depth. You need to understand:

- Why the problem is happening
- What systemic factors or policies are sustaining the problem
- Who the key people or institutions are that could make a difference

This understanding will help you identify your opportunities to have the greatest effect.

Next you need to consider your audience: who needs to hear your message, and what will motivate them to act? Your campaign needs to be engaging to capture people's attention. The way it is worded, the message and the tone should be clear, compelling and authentic.

A good campaign plan outlines:

- Your objectives

- The audience you want to reach

- Your key messages

- The tactics you will use

- The timeline

- The resources available

- How you will measure success

It should also consider the risks, including political sensitivities, reputational issues and the wellbeing of those involved.

Don't forget your ethical and legal responsibilities to ensure that stories and images are used with informed consent and that contributors understand how their words may be used.

Some campaigns rely on shock tactics and use a short message or memorable images to provoke a strong emotional reaction, in the hope this will lead to immediate action. One problem with these types of campaigns is that they can polarise opinion and be divisive, with the risk of alienating the audience, distracting from the message or appearing manipulative. You therefore need to be clear on whether they are appropriate for your audience or message.

Other campaigns use emotional storytelling techniques to build empathy and to invite people to imagine themselves in the pictured scenario. This approach tends to have a broader appeal and foster a sense of connection. It also works well when combined with positivity and humour to create a balanced, uplifting message. However, this type of campaign may not compel action in the same way as a more dramatic one.

Finally, some campaigns produce reports that rely entirely on data and policy messaging. They may include case studies and infographics showing robust socioeconomic analysis. These campaigns can be particularly effective when targeting decision makers.

Tools, tactics and channels

The right tactics for your campaign will depend on your issue, audience and resources. Behind the scenes, many campaigns also rely on research, coalition building and legal work. Examples of campaign tactics include:

- **Direct lobbying.** This approach may involve holding meetings with politicians or senior officials, presenting petitions or submitting policy briefings. It is often most effective when paired with public pressure to demonstrate widespread support.

- **Mobilising communities.** Running workshops, hosting town hall meetings, building alliances with grassroots groups and training peer advocates are examples of how awareness can inspire communities into action.

- **Using social media.** Online platforms allow small organisations to reach wide audiences at relatively low cost. A carefully timed post, powerful image or short video can quickly attract attention.

- **Email campaigns.** Organisations can target supporters with tailored messages and direct them to take action.

- **Creative approaches.** Art installations, poetry, music or theatre can help people connect emotionally with an issue.

- **Public events.** A candlelit vigil, storytelling evening or protest march, for example, is powerful in creating visibility and building community.

Staying legal and managing risk

As an individual, if you're acting in a personal capacity, you have a right to campaign and protest peacefully in the UK, protected by the Human Rights Act 1998, under your rights to free speech and assembly.[45] You can sign and share petitions, attend demonstrations, write to your MP and speak out online or in the media. The only limits apply according to public order laws or where speech crosses into hate, incitement or harassment. The Public Order Act 1986 makes it a criminal offence to use threatening, abusive or insulting words or behaviour if it is likely to cause harassment, alarm or distress.[46] The law also covers stirring up hatred on the grounds of race, religion or sexual orientation.

If your organisation is a registered charity, your campaigning must follow Charity Commission guidance CC9, which provides helpful clarity on what is and isn't allowed.[47] Campaigning must be in line with your charitable purposes, non-party political and compliant with charity law and guidance. In practice, charities are allowed to provide public education, arrange petitions, organise peaceful protests, lobby MPs or ministers and run social media campaigns.

Charities need to be very careful about getting involved in political activity. They are allowed to campaign for a change in government policy or legislation, as long as that change furthers their charitable purposes, but this must never become their sole or continuing activity.

Charities must not support or oppose a particular political party or candidate, suggest that people should vote for a specific party, or donate funds to political parties. During election periods, additional rules under the Lobbying Act may apply if your activities could reasonably be seen as intended to influence voters.[48]

If your organisation is a CIC, CLG or not-for-profit without charitable status, you have more flexibility to engage in political activity and advocacy, including endorsing policies or even criticising political parties, provided you remain within the bounds of company and electoral law. Even here, though, transparency, fairness and accountability matter, particularly if you are receiving public funding. It is important you don't underestimate the reputational risks associated with politics.

Key points

- **Advocacy and influence.** Individual advocacy, collective advocacy, or policy advocacy are different ways in which not-for-profits and charities can influence others for the public good.

- **Campaigning.** Clarifying objectives, identifying the ideal audience, and determining strong messages and tactics are vital steps in crafting an effective campaign to raise public awareness and mobilise support in implementing change.

- **Managing risk.** While individuals have the right to protest peacefully, charities must take care to follow Charity Commission guidelines on campaigning and to take extra care in regard to political activity.

17

Funding

Funding organisations play a vital role in the UK by redistributing money that has been donated, invested or raised from government sources to charities, voluntary groups and community projects. Understanding how the different systems operate is crucial for organisations looking to access funding and to develop strategies that are both realistic and sustainable.

Funding sources

The funds that grant-giving organisations distribute typically come from one or more of the following sources:

- Endowments
- Government and public sector funding
- Philanthropic giving
- Intermediary arrangements

Endowments

Many of the large charitable trusts and foundations are funded through endowments, although they often support smaller organisations as well. Endowments are cash or other valuable assets – such as shares or property – permanently invested to generate an ongoing income from interest, dividends or capital gains. This ensures the original capital is preserved within the investment, while the interest and dividends are used to support the work of the organisation.

Endowments are often invested in the stock market alongside other assets, such as cash, bonds or property, to diversify risk, and are managed by professional investment managers working directly for an investment company. Those investment managers decide which stocks to buy and sell, to balance income generation with protecting the investment against inflation and stock market volatility.

The trustees or directors will make decisions on how the endowment should be invested, to be congruent with the aims of their organisation and governing document.

This is important because companies that trade shares on the stock market do so to raise capital to run the business. Therefore, when an endowment purchases specific shares, they are directly providing financial support to that company, which could be a reputational risk. For example, some organisations may state that they don't want to hold any shares in companies with military contracts or oil interests, while others actively choose to invest in ethical or green funds.

Government and public sector funding

Government funding refers to funds directly controlled by central government departments (like the Department for Education or DCMS), devolved administrations (like the Welsh or Scottish Government) or local government. Public sector funding refers to government money from NHS trusts or integrated care boards, police and crime commissioners, fire and rescue authorities, and state schools or academies.

Government and public sector funding can be given as:

- **Contracts** – legal agreements in which an organisation is commissioned to provide a service on behalf of the public sector
- **Grants** – funds that are awarded to help achieve a shared public goal

You'll find further information on grants at the end of this chapter.

Philanthropic giving

High-net-worth individuals and corporate donors often give to not-for-profit organisations, whether through formal trusts, major one-off gifts or sustained charitable engagement. As these are private arrangements, they often have more flexibility than those of established charities.

While some philanthropists create large endowments to fund long-term work, others give responsively to urgent needs. Some support large infrastructure projects and established institutions, while others focus, for example, on community resilience.

Intermediary arrangements

Some not-for-profits act as intermediaries by receiving funding from public bodies or large foundations and then redistributing it to grassroots organisations. The regranting body typically manages the application process, selects grantees, issues payments and monitors outcomes. It might also provide support, advice or capacity building alongside the funding.

This model is particularly common where the original funder wants to reach small or underrepresented groups but doesn't have the infrastructure to do so directly. The benefit of using trusted intermediaries is that they understand local contexts and can work with groups that may struggle with complex government application systems.

Restricted, unrestricted and designated funds

The terms *restricted* and *unrestricted* are particularly important in not-for-profit organisations, whether giving or receiving funds.

Restricted funds

The principle of restricted funds is simple. When an organisation receives money, the donor is entitled to state the purpose they expect it to be used for. Most larger funders specify the purpose of the grant, thereby creating restricted funding for the recipient.

It is a legal obligation to spend these funds only according to the agreed purpose, and charities specifically must account for restricted funds separately in their financial statements. They are not allowed to borrow from those funds, for example to cover general running costs or unexpected expenses.

Unrestricted funds

These are donations or income that the not-for-profit can use at its discretion to meet any of its objectives.

Examples include general donations from individuals and legacies left without conditions. There are no specific conditions attached to the use of the funds, other than that they must be used in line with the organisation's stated purpose.

Unrestricted income is particularly beneficial because it allows organisations to pay for general overheads like admin staff, utility bills or the development of new services. These are the things that keep the organisation running but which are generally less appealing to funders. However, many funders will allow a proportion of overheads to be included in funding applications (often referred to as a *contribution towards core costs*), and they will expect to see a reasonable budget for these in the application.

Designated funds

Designated funds is an internal term used within organisations for budgeting purposes. It refers to unrestricted funds that the board has set aside for a particular purpose. For example, the board might agree to ringfence a certain amount from general reserves to fund a new website project.

Because designating funds is an internal decision, the designation can be changed by the board, unlike restricted funds, which are legally bound by the donor's instruction.

Match funding

Match funding is the term used when a funder requires you to contribute a certain amount of money or in-kind support to the project as a condition of receiving their grant. Match funding is intended to reduce funder risk while gauging community demand and the longer-term viability of a project.

You may need to raise a fixed percentage of the project costs from other sources, which the funder will then match; or you might be asked to provide organisational resources to the project, for example volunteer time or use of premises, while the funding covers the financial commitments. In many cases you will need to show evidence you have secured your part of the budget before funds are released.

Some funders are more flexible than others, and some are moving away from requiring match funding for smaller amounts, recognising that it can exclude under-resourced groups.

Grants

A grant is a gift of money given for a specific purpose. Grants are fundamentally different to loans and investments, as they are not usually repayable. However, they almost always come with conditions to ensure that public or charitable money is used properly.

Each funding organisation will have a different focus in its grant application process, congruent with the organisation's charitable objectives and governing documents.

Some grants will be advertised and open to all eligible organisations, while others may be by invitation only, for example if previous experience in similar projects is required. Applicants are usually required to submit a funding proposal, which could include:

- Project description

- Budget

- Outline of expected outcomes and details of the organisation

- Why the organisation is best placed to deliver the project

Grant providers evaluate applications based on factors such as fit with priorities, organisational capacity, value for money and potential impact. If the grant evaluation criteria have been provided pre-application, you will need to read them thoroughly and submit information that provides all the information asked for. Many funders actively encourage a pre-application conversation, and this is your opportunity to ask what a good application looks like and what information would make their evaluation process easier.

Grant conditions

Typical conditions include restricted use, meaning the grant can be used to fund only a particular project or purpose, often to strict time limits. Smaller projects may require the full grant to be spent within six to twelve months, whereas larger grants may cover multiple years of funding. Funders may also ask you to acknowledge their support in your publicity and on your website.

When grants are provided to purchase assets such as buildings, vehicles or equipment, there may be additional requirements imposed, such as a requirement to insure the asset and an undertaking not to sell it without prior permission from the grant provider.

If the project is delivered under budget, the funder may request that the surplus funds be returned to them. The funder may sometimes allow the organisation to apply to reallocate the balance to related work, but you must seek permission in writing before doing so.

It is also worth noting that grant agreements usually include clauses that allow the funder to recover money if things go wrong. If you were to spend the grant on ineligible costs or fail to deliver the promised activity, the funder could ask for the money to be returned; or in staged or multiyear grants, they could withhold further payments. In very serious cases, although this happens rarely, they could take legal action against the board.

Project monitoring and evaluation

Once a grant has been awarded, monitoring and evaluation processes are essential to both parties. Funders will usually specify their reporting requirements in the grant documents, and these could include the submission of interim as well as final reports, with evidence such as receipts, photos, testimonials and data. These may be formal written reports or brief updates by phone or email.

Increasingly, funders view evaluation as a mutual learning opportunity. They may invite reflection on what worked and what didn't, and how the experience can shape future projects. For higher-value or long-term grants, funders may request site visits, participant interviews or case studies. This helps humanise the impact data and gives both sides a fuller picture of the successes and challenges.

Good funding applications will consider an exit strategy at the outset and build it into the funding request. This may be to reapply for further charitable funding to scale up the work once the concept has been proven. Alternatively, it could be for a project to become self-sustaining, potentially through commercial or public sector contracts or public donations and service usage.

Key points

- **Funding.** For an organisation to operate, it is of course vital to secure funding, and you will need to gain an understanding of how different systems operate and to investigate any possible funding sources relevant to your organisation.

- **Conditions of funding.** Even with unrestricted funding, it is almost inevitable that you will be required to provide evidence of how donated funds are used in accordance with your stated purposes. Project monitoring and evaluation, including submission of reports on how funding has been used, is vital in maintaining sources of income and identifying areas of potential improvement or shareable best practice.

18

Fundraising

Fundraising is about building relationships, telling your story and asking for support in ways that inspire trust and generosity.

In this chapter we'll explore different types of fundraising and highlight some of the legal requirements. You need to ensure you fully understand the rules relating to your proposed activities and geographical location and seek independent professional advice if necessary.

Fundraising regulators

Fundraising activities in England and Wales are governed primarily by the Charity Commission,[49] and the Fundraising Regulator's Code of Fundraising Practice.[50]

Event licensing under the Licensing Act 2003 may also apply.[51] Charities in Scotland follow the Charity and Trustee Investment (Scotland) Act 2005,[52] and the Civic Government (Scotland) Act 1982.[53]

For Northern Ireland the primary legislation is the Charities Act (Northern Ireland) 2008,[54] and Northern Ireland (Licensing (NI) Order 1996).[55]

Events are also a great way to raise funds. Ticket sales are classed as trading income and are subject to your usual HMRC rules on taxation. A licence is usually required from the licensing authority where the event is taking place for alcohol sales, music and public entertainment. See Chapter 14 for more information.

There are regional differences between the countries of the UK and the counties within each, so I will give only an overview of general principles and how to confirm which regulations apply to your own circumstances.

Only registered charities can call themselves charities or offer Gift Aid.

Organisations do not need to be registered charities to fundraise, but they must be transparent about where the money is going and must not mislead donors.

The table below gives a quick reference summary of the legal regulator for each country and activity.

	England	Wales	Scotland	Northern Ireland
Fundraising regulation	Fundraising Regulator	Fundraising Regulator	Fundraising Regulator	Voluntary registration with Fundraising Regulator
Charity regulation	Charity Commission for England and Wales	Charity Commission for England and Wales	OSCR	CCNI
Lottery legislation	Gambling Act 2005	Gambling Act 2005	Gambling Act 2005	Betting, Gaming, Lotteries and Amusements (NI) Order 1985
Lottery licensing	Gambling Commission/ local authority	Gambling Commission/ local authority	Gambling Commission/ local authority	Local authority (no Gambling Commission role)
Incidental lottery	No licence needed if held during an event	No licence needed if held during an event	No licence needed if held during an event	No licence needed if held during an event
Small society lottery (advance tickets)	Register with local authority; no Gambling Commission licence	Register with local authority; no Gambling Commission licence	Register with local authority; no Gambling Commission licence	Register with local council
Customer lottery	Business run, strict conditions apply	Same as England	Same as England	Not permitted under NI law
Online or national lotteries	Gambling Commission licence required	Business run, strict conditions apply	Business run, strict conditions apply	Generally prohibited or complex under NI law
Collection tins in private premises	Allowed with premises owner's permission, sealed and labelled tins required	Allowed with premises owner's permission, sealed and labelled tins required	Allowed with premises owner's permission, sealed and labelled tins required	Allowed with premises owner's permission, sealed and labelled tins required

	England	Wales	Scotland	Northern Ireland
Public collections (street/doorstep)	Local council licence required	Local council licence required	Permit required from local council (Civic Government (Scotland) Act 1982)	PSNI or council licence required (Northern Ireland: Street and House To House Collections Act 1962)[56]
Eligibility to fundraise	Any not-for-profit; must not mislead about charitable status	Any not-for-profit; must not mislead about charitable status	Any not-for-profit; must not mislead about charitable status	Any not-for-profit; must not mislead about charitable status
Can Gift Aid be claimed?	Only by HMRC-recognised charities or CASCs	Only by HMRC-recognised charities or CASCs	Only by HMRC-recognised charities or CASCs	Only by HMRC-recognised charities or CASCs
Data protection	UK GDPR and Data Protection Act 2018, regulated by ICO	UK GDPR and Data Protection Act 2018, regulated by ICO	UK GDPR and Data Protection Act 2018, regulated by ICO	UK GDPR and Data Protection Act 2018, regulated by ICO
Event ticket sales	Trading income, covered by HMRC regulations	Trading income, covered by HMRC regulations	Trading income, covered by HMRC regulations	Trading income, covered by HMRC regulations
Event entertainment and music	Local councils under the Licensing Act 2003	Local councils under the Licensing Act 2003	Local councils under the Civic Government (Scotland) Act 1982	Magistrates' courts under the Local Government (Miscellaneous Provisions) (NI) Order 1985
Event alcohol sales	Local councils under the Licensing Act 2003	Local councils under the Licensing Act 2003	Local councils under the Licensing (Scotland) Act 2005	Magistrates' courts under the Northern Ireland (Licensing (NI) Order 1996)

Fundraising activities

There are multiple different ways to fundraise, but activities that involve asking for money from members of the public are highly regulated. Here I'll cover the main categories you might like to explore for your own fundraising activities.

Lotteries

Under UK law, any fundraising that involves paying for a ticket in return for a chance to win a prize is considered a form of lottery, even if it's called something else such as a raffle, prize draw or sweepstake. Any lottery falls under the rules of the Gambling Act 2005,[57] which is regulated by the Gambling Commission.[58] This is applies regardless of how small or informal the fundraiser is.

A lottery has three defining features, and all three criteria must apply:

1. There is a payment to enter

2. There is at least one prize

3. The winners are chosen at random[59]

Lotteries in the UK can be run only to support charities and other good causes, with the proceeds being specifically used for non-commercial purposes. Private profit-making lotteries are specifically prohibited under UK law.

The Gambling Commission officially recognises seven main types of lottery in the UK, as shown in the table below, not all of which are relevant to fundraising.

Lottery type	Who can run it	Licence or registration	Purpose
Large society lottery	Charities or non-commercial societies	Gambling Commission licence	Fundraising (proceeds exceeding £20k per draw or £250k/year)
Small society lottery	Charities or non-commercial societies	Local authority registration	Fundraising (proceeds lower than £20k per draw and £250k/year)
Local authority lottery	Local councils	Gambling Commission licence	Local funding for public services
Workplace lottery	Employers, for employees only	No licence needed, but it must meet conditions	Employee engagement or entertainment
Residents' lottery	Residents of a single premises	No licence needed, but it must meet conditions	Fun or local improvements
Customer lottery	Businesses (for customers only)	No licence needed, but it is heavily restricted	Promotion or entertainment, not fundraising

Lottery type	Who can run it	Licence or registration	Purpose
Incidental lottery	Anyone, as part of a non-commercial event	No licence needed	Fundraising or fun at events

The ones most relevant to fundraising in the not-for-profit space are society lotteries and incidental lotteries.

Society lotteries

These can be defined as either small or large, with the definition and regulations being determined by the proceeds raised. With small society lotteries, the maximum proceeds from a single draw cannot exceed £20,000, and if multiple draws take place across the year, the total proceeds cannot exceed £250,000. Each ticket can cost no more than £2, and at least 20% of proceeds must go to the stated cause. Tickets must show the name of the organisation, the date of the draw, the price of the ticket, and the name and address of the promoter (which may not be the organisation itself). Large society lotteries raise proceeds in excess of £20,000 per draw or £250,000 per year and require a Gambling Commission licence. They are more often used by grant-giving organisations such as the National Lottery, who then distribute funds to smaller not-for-profits and charities.

Incidental lotteries

The most informal type, incidental lotteries are commonly used for community or charity fundraising at events. They must be held during an event, hence the term incidental, and are often seen at school fetes, community fun days and quiz nights. No registration or licence is required and, while there is no limit on ticket prices or prize value, they must be 'reasonable'. However, ticket selling and the prize draw must take place only during the event. Advance ticket sales are strictly prohibited, and you cannot roll over prizes or sell tickets online. If you want to sell tickets in advance, you must first register the draw with the local authority as a small society lottery.

Collecting tins

Using collecting tins or buckets is a common way to raise funds. Your organisation does not need to be a registered charity to collect in this way, but non-charitable entities must be clear not to mislead donors.

You must get the owner's permission to place a tin in private premises such as on a shop counter or in a pub or office. No formal licence is required for private sites, but the Fundraising Regulator guidance states that the collecting container must be labelled, numbered and sealed to prevent tampering.[60] The container should also be clearly labelled with the name of the organisation for which you are collecting funds.[61] Tins should be collected regularly and processed promptly.

For collections taking place in a public area or door to door, organisations need to apply for a licence from either the local authority or, if the collection is in Greater London, from the Metropolitan Police.

Direct debit fundraising

This method often uses trained fundraisers to approach members of the public in busy areas, such as high streets and shopping centres, and invite them to make a one-off donation or regular gift via direct debit.

Unlike street cash collections, direct debit fundraising does not require a licence because it is not a request for immediate payment. However, to protect the public, many councils and private sites have measures in place to control the volume and frequency of this type of fundraising.

The Charity Commission and the Fundraising Regulator provide detailed guidance on the legal responsibilities and standards that apply to face-to-face fundraising, and organisations must follow the Code of Fundraising Practice.[62] This includes guidance on:

- Treating the public with respect
- Clearly identifying the charity
- The requirement not to apply pressure or make misleading statements
- Offering accessible and accurate information about how donations will be used

Fundraisers must not continue speaking to someone who has clearly indicated they are not interested, and special care must be taken when approaching any possible donor who may be in vulnerable circumstances or need extra care and support to make an informed decision.

Some charities include an ethical fundraising statement on their website or in their fundraising literature, outlining how they train and supervise fundraisers, how they handle complaints and how they honour donor preferences.

Donations and legacies

Donations are gifts of money, goods or services that are freely given, with no expectation of receiving anything in return. Legacies are gifts left in individuals' wills.

Legacies can be left to individuals, charities, trusts, not-for-profit companies, unincorporated associations or even informal groups of individuals. However, legacies given to registered charities enjoy tax benefits for the donor that are not available to other organisations.[63] These can help the donor with inheritance tax planning as well as supporting a good cause.

The majority of charitable legacies result from encouragement by the not-for-profit through newsletters, legacy promotion platforms (like Remember a Charity or Will Aid) and advertising campaigns. Legacy fundraising is about telling your story and showing supporters that your work is worth investing in, both now and beyond their lifetime.

Payment to fundraisers

There are times when engaging a professional fundraiser can significantly improve your organisation's results, but payments made to employ fundraisers must be reasonable, proportionate and in the best interests of your organisation and its beneficiaries.

There are several common models of payment. Fixed fees, such as a day rate or project fee, are popular and allow simple budgeting. However, you pay the same amount, whether or not the income generated meets expectations.

Performance-related pay and commission-based models offer payment based on the funds raised. While they can incentivise high performance, fundraisers may feel pressured to use pushy tactics, and your reputation could be damaged if the public suspect fundraisers are motivated by financial reward.

Key points

- **Fundraising activities.** There are many ways charities can raise operational funds, including lotteries, collecting tins, direct debit fundraising, legacies and events. Your organisation must be aware of all potential regulations and requirements in order to operate legally and avoid reputational damage.

- **Regulations.** Whatever type of fundraising activity you're planning, it is likely to be subject to regulations. Check the relevant guidance from the Charity Commission, the Fundraising Regulator, the Gambling Commission or your local authority.

- **Professional fundraisers.** Engaging professional fundraisers can often raise more money for a charity than the salary or one-off payments made to the fundraisers. Caution is vital, though, to protect existing funding and your organisation's reputation.

PART FOUR
GOVERNANCE

Governance is the framework that supports everything else your organisation does. It's how you ensure your organisation is ethical, legally compliant, financially responsible and aligned with its core purpose. In Part Four we focus on the structures, systems and principles that will keep your not-for-profit on track.

I begin with ethical leadership, transparency, accountability and environmental responsibility as markers of a well-run organisation. You'll learn how to identify and manage conflicts of interest, embed sustainable practices in your operations and create a culture that reflects your values at every level.

After that we look at different types of meetings, their functions and how to make them inclusive, focused and productive. I'll also cover how to take accurate minutes, record decisions and track actions effectively.

Next we explore finance and budgets, how to plan effectively and how to identify potential problems early on. I'll also signpost in regard to essential tax and benefit topics, including VAT, corporation tax, PAYE and Gift Aid, so you know where to look for further advice and guidance.

Running a not-for-profit always involves some level of risk, whether to your people, reputation, assets or data. I'll introduce risk management in a practical, proportionate way, helping you assess potential threats and put sensible measures in place. I'll look at data protection (including GDPR), record keeping and document retention as well as safeguarding – all topics that are increasingly important and closely regulated.

Our final chapter focuses on monitoring and evaluating impact, and the essential tasks of review, reflection and renewal. In the day-to-day pressures of running services and balancing budgets, it's easy to lose sight of the bigger picture. Pausing to evaluate what is and isn't working is one of the most valuable habits you can develop.

19

Governance, Ethics And Sustainability

This chapter explores the board's responsibilities for governance and safeguarding and explores how to lead ethically, manage conflicts of interest and make decisions with long-term impact in mind.

Strategic governance

Governance involves setting the strategic direction for the organisation, ensuring legal and regulatory compliance while managing risks and overseeing performance. In a well-governed organisation individuals know who is responsible for what, how decisions are made, and how problems are identified and dealt with.

Governance is the responsibility of the board of directors or trustees. Their role is to safeguard the organisation's purpose, reputation and assets. The specific duties depend on the organisation's legal form, but the principles are broadly consistent across structures.

The board must:

- Comply with the law and the organisation's governing document

- Use the organisation's resources wisely to avoid undue risk

- Act in the organisation's best interests

- Be answerable to beneficiaries, funders, regulators and the wider public

Importantly, the board is collectively responsible. Even if individual trustees take on specific roles, decisions need to be made jointly and documented properly. Minutes of meetings are a key part of demonstrating that governance is being properly exercised.

One of the most common governance risks, particularly in small organisations, is informality and the blurring of responsibilities. For example, decisions might be made by a small group without proper consultation or documentation, or a staff member might be allowed to make policy decisions without board oversight.

Good practice guidance recommends that you review your governing document annually and keep role descriptions up to date, to ensure everyone understands their legal duties. You need to create simple policies for delegation, conflicts of interest and risk management; and schedule regular board meetings with clear agendas, minutes and actions. You should also carry out a board skills audit to identify gaps and support succession planning.

Governance in respect of safeguarding

Safeguarding means protecting a person's right to live in safety, free from abuse and neglect. It applies particularly, but not exclusively, to children and adults at risk. The board plays a critical role in ensuring the organisation's safeguarding culture is effective, proactive and legally compliant.

The responsibilities vary slightly, depending on the legal form and regulatory framework of the organisation, but some duties are universal across England, Wales, Scotland and Northern Ireland.

In England and Wales the Charity Commission guidance expects trustees to follow all statutory guidance, good practice guidance and legislation relevant to their organisation.[64] This includes:

- Having appropriate policies in place and ensuring they are followed

- Checking that people are suitable to act in their roles

- Having a clear system for reporting concerns to relevant agencies at the earliest opportunity

In Scotland the OSCR echoes these principles, stating, 'It's important that charities consider how to promote wellbeing and welfare of all the individuals they work with.'[65]

In Northern Ireland the CCNI advises that 'Charity trustees must consider safeguarding elements of service delivery, in supporting projects, working with partners and employing staff.'[66]

Core elements

The following elements are core to safeguarding good practice, regardless of the country in which you operate:

- **Policy.** The board must ensure that the safeguarding policy sets out procedures for recognising and reporting concerns, including whistleblowing, and the policy should be tailored to the organisation's specific activities and risks.

- **People at risk.** Organisations working with children and vulnerable adults need to appoint a designated safeguarding lead – often a member of staff or senior volunteer. All staff and volunteers, including board members, should receive safeguarding training appropriate to their role.

- **Practices.** Safe recruitment practices should be embedded in the organisation. These practices include DBS checks where applicable, references, and role-specific safeguarding questions at interview.

- **Transparency.** The organisation's culture should support openness and active listening, both to deter poor behaviour and to make early reporting of concerns easy. Boards should receive regular reports on safeguarding, particularly around incidents, near misses and audits of compliance.

- **Regulation.** Boards must ensure they are compliant with the framework relevant to their jurisdiction. Multination charities must take care to apply the correct legislation in each area.

Ethical leadership and decision making

At the heart of ethical leadership lies a legal and moral duty to act in the best interests of the organisation, and the board are bound by company and/or charity law to remain independent in their judgement. The principle applies to staff and volunteers as well, particularly when they are involved in financial decisions or service planning.

Acting in the organisation's best interest means looking at each decision through the lens of what will best serve the organisation's purpose and the people it supports, instead of what is easiest or cheapest, or best for the individuals making the decision.

Board members should always be willing to challenge decisions that appear to benefit individuals over the organisation as a whole, and staff and volunteers need to feel confident in raising concerns if something does not feel right. Acting in the organisation's best interests sometimes means asking difficult questions and creating a culture where doing so is welcomed.

Sometimes organisations are faced with decisions that bring about ethical dilemmas. Imagine an environmental organisation has been offered funding from a donor whose trust fund is invested in oil and gas stocks. Accepting the funds would allow the organisation to deliver crucial services but at the cost of potential reputational damage.

It helps to have a shared process for thinking through ethical choices. You can start by returning to the organisation's charitable aims and assessing whether any decision clearly furthers those aims and aligns with the organisation's values and long-term reputation. Consider who might be affected – beneficiaries, funders, staff and the wider community – and whether they should be consulted. It can help to reflect on how the decision will be recorded and whether you would be happy to explain it publicly.

Some organisations adopt simple ethical decision-making frameworks, which include structured sets of questions to work through, while others might establish working groups or staff panels to bring in multiple perspectives.

Identifying and managing conflicts of interest

A conflict of interest arises when someone involved in the organisation has a competing interest that could affect their impartiality, whether through a personal relationship, a business interest or another role. These situations are not usually deliberate, and they're not inherently a cause for concern. However, if they are not handled openly and fairly, they can compromise decision making, erode trust and potentially breach legal obligations.

The ethical approach is to recognise and manage conflicts transparently.

Conflict of interest practices are partly covered by the legal requirement to act in the best interest of the organisation and backed up by the Bribery Act 2010 (section 7), which introduces the offence of 'failure of commercial organisations to prevent bribery'.[67] The defence is to show that the organisation 'had in place adequate procedures designed to prevent [...] such conduct'.

It is best practice to keep a register of interests that is reviewed regularly and updated whenever someone's circumstances change. Everyone in a position of influence within the organisation, particularly board members and senior staff, must declare any roles, relationships or business links that could give rise to a conflict.

The register must be updated and reviewed regularly by a senior member of staff or board member to ensure no mutually exclusive conflicts have been declared that would have the power to prejudice someone's judgement to the extent that they could not be involved in the organisation. One extreme example could be someone with a close family connection to a close competitor of the organisation.

Declarations of interest should be made at the beginning of each meeting where a conflicted subject is due to be discussed. The conflict should be noted against the relevant agenda item(s), and the individual with the conflict should remove themselves from both the discussion and the vote.

The same process should be followed if a relevant item is raised during the course of the meeting, at which point the individual should immediately declare the conflict and excuse themselves.

Embedding sustainability in operations

Sustainability is crucial to the success of an organisation. While financial sustainability is obvious, it is also important to consider environmental responsibility and ethical practice.

An environmentally responsible organisation considers the impact of its decisions on both people and the planet. This could include reducing energy consumption by investing in energy-efficient lighting, turning off equipment when it is not in use and using green energy suppliers. Digital systems can reduce paper use, but they also come with their own carbon footprint. This can be mitigated by cutting out unnecessary email traffic, selecting eco-friendly web hosting services and using effective digital destruction processes to reduce storage requirements.

When organising events, the organisation can choose venues that prioritise environmental sustainability. You can offer vegetarian or vegan catering options, avoid single-use plastics and provide recycling facilities. You could also consider how your travel policies affect emissions and whether you could hold more meetings online or encourage the use of public transport, cycles or car sharing.

Sustainable procurement means buying from suppliers who reflect your values. This might include local businesses, social enterprises, B Corps or cooperatives.

You can ask suppliers about their labour practices, emissions targets and environmental policies, and review your banking arrangements to check whether your funds are contributing to ethical investment or supporting fossil fuels or human rights abuses.

Embedding sustainability is a team effort. Appointing a sustainability champion or working group, building goals into your strategic plan and publicly reporting progress can all help make environmental care part of everyday decision making.

Key points

- **Strategic governance.** Good governance requires clear roles, documented decisions and meetings, and regular reviews of policies. The board is responsible for setting direction and protecting the organisation through robust governance practices.

- **Safeguarding.** The board plays a critical role in ensuring the organisation's safeguarding culture is effective, proactive and legally compliant, according to the regulators of the geographic areas in which the organisation is active.

- **Ethical leadership.** All members of the organisation have a legal and moral duty to act in the best interests of the organisation, and the board are bound by company and charity law to remain independent.

- **Conflicts of interest.** Any potential conflicts must be declared, recorded and transparently managed to ensure decisions are made in the best interests of the organisation.

- **Sustainability.** Financial, ethical and environmental sustainability are crucial to the long-term success of an organisation.

20
Effective Meetings

Meetings are an essential part of governance and planning, but to be effective they need to be purposeful and inclusive.

This chapter explores the different types of meetings common in the not-for-profit sector, from board meetings and AGMs to working groups and staff meetings. It also offers guidance on how to prepare, run and follow up, to ensure meetings are efficient, inclusive and effective.

Understanding meeting types

There are four main types of formal meetings held at not-for-profit organisations:

1. Board meetings

2. General meetings – AGMs and EGMs

3. Strategy meetings

4. Tactical meetings

Board meetings

Regular board or trustee meetings are central to governance of the organisation. This is where policy decisions are made, risks are reviewed and budgets are monitored. Board meetings should be held often enough for the board to be able to set the policy on key issues but not so regularly that there is no time for implementation between meetings. The majority of organisations find bimonthly or quarterly meetings a reasonable schedule.

It is good practice to plan the dates for these meetings up to a year in advance to ensure board members can plan attendance around their other commitments.

General meetings – AGMs and EGMs

The governing document of the organisation usually requires an AGM that follows strict procedural rules and is open to all members. The statutory business requires a vote on the appointment of any new or renewing board members.

Many organisations' governing documents also require members to approve the financial accounts. Although the requirement to present accounts at general meetings was dropped for private limited companies by the Companies Act 2006 and has been removed from the Companies House model articles, it has not been removed from the requirements of companies formed prior to the updated legislation. If you want to remove the requirement from your governing document, you will need to put a motion forward at a general meeting for a vote by members.

The AGM is also an opportunity for the board to provide an update on the work of the organisation over the past year as well as sharing plans for the future.

The governing document should state:

- The maximum time allowed between AGMs
- How much notice should be given of the date (the *calling notice*)
- How members will be informed
- The required quorum

When drafting or amending the governing document, it is important to set the quorum for voting at a specific number or a percentage of members you can easily reach. The number should, though, not be set so low that important or controversial decisions could be made by a small minority.

The calling notice should include details of how and when members can submit items for the agenda and details of how members can put themselves forward for board roles.

If a specific issue arises that requires a vote by members, the board can call an EGM, which follows the same convening rules as the AGM.

Strategy meetings

Strategy meetings are arranged to set the strategic direction of the organisation, often over multiple years. They are intended for high-level, big-picture decisions rather than focusing on how things might work in practice.

Strategy meetings may revisit the vision and mission of the organisation, or consider the possibility of strategic partnerships and how those might impact the organisation. These meetings are held irregularly – at most annually. Occasionally, though, if a significant change of course is being considered, it may take more than one session to finalise the strategy.

Tactical meetings

Tactical meetings, for example involving a finance committee or fundraising sub group, will take place regularly. These are more practical meetings for planning day-to-day activity and assigning tasks to staff and volunteers.

The timing of tactical meetings will vary depending on the size and complexity of the organisation and whether there is a specific challenge coming up, for example financial year end or a large fundraising event. Tactical meetings are internal, not referred to in the governing documents and do not require specific notification periods or attendance quorums

Meeting quorum and voting

The meeting quorum is the minimum number of voting individuals required to legally conduct the business of the organisation, ie to reach valid decisions. The governing document should specify how to organise formal meetings (the AGM and board meetings), including how much notice is required and how many of the board members need to be present to form a quorum. It is often beneficial to require at least one of the specified officers be present so the document can state, *The quorum for meetings is 50% of the board, including at least one of the posts of chair, secretary or treasurer.*

The governing document will also detail how any decisions should be made, for example if a show of hands is sufficient or a secret ballot is required, and whether a simple majority or specific percentage will carry the motion. There should also be instructions on how to move forward in the event of a tied vote. For example, the meeting chair may have a casting vote, or the vote could be extended to those not present at the meeting.

It is also important to check that your governing document allows the use of online meeting technology, following the explosion in its use during Covid. Many documents already specify that trustees and directors do not need to be physically present in the same location for a meeting to be valid, but if this clause is not present, decisions made at online meetings may not be valid.

Planning and facilitating inclusive meetings

A well-prepared agenda is central to a successful meeting. There is often a standard agenda template for each formal meeting to ensure no area of business is overlooked, and then additional specific items are added under each heading (finance, operations, governance, etc). Ideally, at least for the more formal meetings such as the AGM or strategy meetings, the agenda should be drafted collaboratively by the chair and secretary (or CEO in staff-led organisations) and circulated at least a week in advance, along with any supporting documents. These might include the previous meeting's minutes, financial reports, policy drafts and project updates.

Each agenda item should be categorised to show whether it is for information, discussion or decision. This helps participants prepare and focus their attention. Allocating estimated timings to agenda items also helps keep the meeting on track. Including a brief introduction for each item to explain why it has been included improves clarity and encourages informed contributions.

Meetings should start with a welcome from the chair, introductions if needed and an outline of the agenda. The chair is responsible for keeping to the agenda and timings, bringing discussions back to the main subject and moving them on where necessary. The chair is also responsible for ensuring all viewpoints are heard so that the meeting is not monopolised by one or two participants.

Minutes and action logs

Particularly in the case of the more formal meetings at any not-for-profit, it's vital that clear records are kept of the important points discussed and any decisions made.

Minutes

Minutes are produced from the detailed notes taken during a meeting and provide the formal record of what was discussed, what was decided and what will happen next. They must be agreed as accurate by those present at the meeting then stored as a legal record of the business conducted.

Before the advent of computers and electronic filing, organisations used to record minutes in ledgers, and you can sometimes still find these stored in archives on the premises or in libraries.

Meeting minutes should:

- Capture key points, note major contributions (without attributing every comment) and provide a clear record of all decisions taken

- Include the date, time and location of the meeting, a list of attendees and apologies, any declarations of interest, and a summary of each agenda item

- Record decisions, including the wording of any resolutions passed alongside a note of the voting result, eg '5:3 in favour' or 'unanimous', and details of the actions agreed, including the name of the person responsible and a deadline if applicable

Minutes should *not* include unnecessary detail, side conversations or anything that might breach confidentiality. They are a public record for many organisations, particularly charities, and should be written clearly and respectfully.

Draft minutes should be circulated within one or two weeks of the meeting, ideally by the secretary, and attendees should be invited to suggest corrections before the next meeting. At the start of the next meeting, minutes need to be formally approved by those present and recorded as such.

Action logs

An action log complements the minutes. It is a running list of the actions agreed at meetings, who is responsible and when the actions should be completed. This log can be kept in a spreadsheet, a shared document or a project management tool. It should be updated after each meeting and completed items archived. The log is often used as a standing item at future meetings to ensure continuity and accountability.

A good action log helps maintain momentum between meetings and ensures everyone knows what they have agreed to do. It also supports chairs and project leads in following up without micro managing.

Key points

- **The point of meetings.** Not-for-profits are required to hold AGMs to allow members to vote on key decisions and board elections (and often to oversee accounts), and EGMs can be called for additional constitutional decisions throughout the year. Strategic and tactical meetings have different but vital purposes, in managing governance, compliance and day-to-day operations.

- **Facilitation.** Formal meetings require clear agendas, supporting documents and inclusive participation.

- **Record keeping.** Accurate minutes and action logs are essential to document decisions and track progress between meetings. The previous meeting's minutes will be reviewed by attendees of the next meeting, thereby maintaining accountability and continuity.

21

Managing Finance And Budgets

There is a lot of terminology in organisational finance, and this chapter is designed to demystify the various concepts while giving you the words and phrases to conduct further independent research.

Legally, the board are responsible for the financial management of the organisation. They must not agree to expenditure or investment that could put the organisation at financial risk, unless that risk is well managed and in the organisation's best interests (for example, through agreeing to debt via a bank loan). They must ensure that money is used in line with any restrictions and that appropriate records are kept. In addition, project income and expenditure often needs to be reported separately to funders and included in the organisation's annual accounts.[68]

Every organisation needs good bookkeeping systems and processes in place to record income and expenditure throughout the year. It is good practice to have financial policies and procedures covering areas such as two-person authorisation for spending, spending limits, petty cash, financial controls and fraud prevention. A reserves policy – detailing how much money you keep in reserve and why – is also vital.

Financial affairs are heavily regulated, with penalties for missed deadlines and incorrect submissions. If your organisation is incorporated, you are required to submit annual accounts to Companies House and/or the Charity Commission. If you are required to register for VAT, returns must normally be submitted quarterly. I would always recommend engaging an accountant and trained bookkeeper to ensure compliance and to demonstrate that the board are upholding their fiduciary responsibilities.

Understanding income and expenditure

Not-for-profit organisations receive income and pay expenses in the same way as any other business. Good record keeping is vital owing to the specific differentiation and classification of funds in the sector and company and charity reporting requirements.

Income

Not-for-profit organisations can have a wide range of income streams. It is important to accurately record the source of each funding stream (for example, donations, grants, events), including whether the funds are restricted or unrestricted and any additional spending conditions, such as time limits or geographical restrictions.

Expenses

In accounting, payments to suppliers are classified as either direct expenses or overheads. Direct expenses are costs that can be allocated directly to a particular project, service or activity. They may include venue hire or catering costs for an event.

In contrast, overheads, also known as indirect costs, are the ongoing costs of running your organisation. Overheads include office rent, broadband, utilities, insurance, administrative salaries and accountancy fees.

Chart of accounts

Financial information is recorded in a chart of accounts, which is a list of all the income and expenditure categories your organisation uses, grouped into logical sections such as income, direct costs, overheads, assets, liabilities and reserves.

Each item in the chart of accounts is given a nominal (number) code, also called an account code. Your chart of accounts should have enough separate income and expenditure categories to allow meaningful reporting and analysis but not so many that it becomes too complex.

Reconciliation

You should regularly perform reconciliation – matching your bank transactions to your accounting records – to make sure no transactions have been missed or recorded incorrectly.

This is particularly important when accounting software is used in maintaining accounts, as it creates reports using numerical ranges. If something is in the wrong section, eg income in an expenditure range, it will introduce errors into the accounting figures.

Cash flow

Cash flow refers to the timing of income and expenditure and is as important as the totals. A healthy budget on paper can still cause problems if the expected income does not arrive before the bills need to be paid.

Creating and monitoring budgets

A budget shows expected income and planned expenditure over a defined period. Your organisation will have an overall annual budget as well as project-specific budgets and perhaps multiyear projections for long-term planning.

The annual budget should include all expected income and expenditure, noting restricted and unrestricted funds. It should detail the overheads alongside separate project costs so it is clear what funds are committed, what might be subject to change, and what assumptions have been made (eg expected fundraising totals).

Once the budget is agreed, regular monitoring is crucial. Actual income and expenditure should be compared with the budget and any significant variances should be explained. Simple management accounts – short reports showing the financial position against budget and cash flow – should be shared with the board and senior staff to support decision making.

There are two methods of accounting used in the UK:

- **Cash accounting** – records income and expenses when money changes hands, for example, when you receive income or pay a bill

- **Accrual accounting** – records income and expenses when they are earned or incurred, even if the money has not yet moved

Accrual accounting is the standard method because it gives a more accurate picture of financial health over time, and it is an HMRC requirement for incorporated organisations.

Project budgets

Project budgets allow the organisation to assess whether a project is affordable, sustainable and in the best interests of the organisation.

You will need to know both the costs of getting the project started and the ongoing costs, so that these can be balanced against the expected income. It is good practice to include your assumptions so you can assess the risks and viability of the project.

Project cash flow figures are vital in showing the expected timing of income and expenditure and ensuring you will have the money when you need it, for example to cover upfront costs or delayed income. The cash flow reports will also identify any overspend or underspend early and allow corrective action if necessary.

Event budgets

Some organisations will use profits from one area of business to offset event costs, either for marketing or as a membership benefit, while some events are designed to generate a profit.

There are two approaches to budget setting:

1. Starting by deciding how much money you want to spend and then designing an appropriate event within that budget

2. Designing the event first and then working out how much it will cost to deliver

Some of the largest costs to think about are venue hire, catering costs, audio visual equipment, speaker fees, entertainment and subsidised places for guests of honour and staff.

The breakeven point is where the income and expenditure are equal, resulting in a net zero cost. It is good practice to work out your breakeven figures on approximately 60–80% attendance. It's worth noting that free-to-attend events have significantly higher drop-out rates than those with expensive pre-purchased tickets.

It is advisable to project a range of scenarios in the planning stage, changing the variables on costs and ticket prices until you find an offering that meets your objectives and a ticket price that your audience will comfortably pay.

The table below gives an example budget planning exercise.

Every event should have a contingency fund. This is money you don't expect to spend but is easily available should it be required.

You can purchase specialist event insurance policies that will pay out if the event is cancelled. It is important to check the small print carefully to make sure any policy meets your requirements, and you will need to notify the insurer of any changes to the proposed event as soon as they are made. Even with valid insurance, you may incur costs that you need to cover from your contingency before a claim is settled.

Scenario	Ticket price	Event costs	Breakeven sales needed	Tickets actually sold	Total income	Profit
High ticket price	£50	£1,000	20 tickets	30 tickets	£1,500	£500
Low ticket price	£20	£1,000	50 tickets	60 tickets	£1,200	£200

Taxes and financial benefits

There are four main taxes and financial benefits relevant to charities:

1. VAT

2. Corporation tax

3. PAYE

4. Gift Aid

VAT

The implementation of VAT within a not-for-profit can be complex. If the taxable turnover of a for-profit business exceeds the VAT threshold (£90,000, as of 2024/25), it must register for VAT. While it must then charge VAT on all its sales, it is allowed to reclaim VAT paid on goods and services used to make taxable supplies.

However, in not-for-profit organisations certain activities can be zero-rated or exempt from VAT, which reduces the taxable turnover, even when the actual turnover is above the registration threshold. Goods and services that qualify for the zero rate include advertising and items for collecting donations, resuscitation training models and goods for disabled people.[69]

Furthermore, if organisations sell some items or services that are taxable, in addition to their core exempt services, they may be eligible for partial exemption, which allows the organisation to reclaim a percentage of its purchase VAT.

The UK has multiple rates of VAT, including standard rate, reduced rate, zero rate and exempt. Expenditure must be recorded against the correct rate to avoid overclaiming and risking financial penalties or criminal prosecution.

Corporation tax

Corporation tax is paid by organisations on their taxable profits. Profits are the money left over from income after allowable expenses (those incurred wholly and exclusively for the business) are deducted. Taxable profits are further adjusted by tax reliefs like capital allowances, which have strict rules attached.

Most not-for-profit organisations are exempt from paying corporation tax on profits from membership or charitable activities, grants, donations and some investment income. However, where an organisation provides services that are not exempt, for example sales from a profit-making gift shop or training to non-members, the profit generated from these activities is subject to normal corporation tax rules.

Even if there is no tax to pay, your accountant must still submit an annual corporation tax return (CT600) within the standard deadlines.

PAYE

PAYE is a compulsory scheme for deducting tax and national insurance contributions from employed staff at source. The level of deductions depends on the individual's circumstances, including their tax-free allowance and their annual earnings. The calculations are made each pay period, and the employer is required to send the deductions directly to HMRC, along with any employer national insurance due.

Gift Aid

Gift Aid is a scheme that allows charities and CASCs throughout the UK to claim an extra 25p for every £1 donated by a UK taxpayer. As the donation is dependent on the donor's tax status, the donor must complete a Gift Aid declaration confirming they understand they must have paid at least as much income tax as the charity is reclaiming; otherwise, they may be liable to repay the difference to HMRC. Gift Aid cannot be reclaimed on company donations or on donations from individuals who don't pay tax in the UK.

Key points

- **Accountability.** The responsibility for management of funds, risk and compliance lies with the organisation's board. Clear policies and accurate bookkeeping are essential.

- **Budgets.** Organisations must prepare budgets for annual overheads and all projects and track income and expenditure. Cash flow, reconciliation and financial reporting are all vital components in the successful running of any organisation.

- **Taxes and financial benefits.** Charities must pay particular attention to VAT, corporation tax,

PAYE (in case of paid employees) and Gift Aid, to avoid penalties for non-compliance and to take advantage of any financial relief.

22

Risk Management And Data Protection

This chapter explores the principles of risk management as well as your responsibilities around data protection, including GDPR compliance.

Risk management

Risk management is the process of identifying and assessing potential events or situations that could negatively affect your organisation and then taking proportionate steps to reduce the likelihood or impact of those risks.

You can't eliminate risk, but being aware of it allows you to make informed choices. While the board can delegate the day-to-day activities of risk management, they can't delegate their responsibility in overall management.

Best practice includes:

- Creating a risk register (a document that lists the risks, their likelihood and how you'll manage them)

- Compiling a business continuity plan

- Documenting your business continuity management process

- Having contingency plans in place for risks like IT failure, staff absence or loss of income

- Having an overarching disaster recovery plan in case of temporary or permanent loss of premises or a key member of staff

- Regularly reviewing policies

- Conducting regular training and supervision for staff and volunteers

Business continuity covers how an organisation plans to keep its essential functions running during and after a disruption. A business continuity plan usually maps out critical activities, identifies the resources needed to maintain them, and sets out how the organisation will adapt to keep services going with as little interruption as possible.

Disaster recovery, on the other hand, is more specific. It focuses on how to get back to normal once a disaster has happened. It often refers to the technical and operational processes for restoring systems, data and infrastructure after a major incident.

The International Organization for Standardisation (ISO) standard 31000 deals specifically with organisational risk. It includes a useful 'Principles, Framework and Process' diagram, which is published online as a free resource.[70]

Risk register

The risk register is the central record of the risks your organisation faces, together with an assessment of their likelihood and impact, and the actions being taken to manage them. It provides a structured way of capturing information, ensuring that risks are documented, visible and capable of being monitored over time. For not-for-profit organisations, this might include financial risks relating to the loss of a funding stream, operational risks like an IT system failure, compliance risks arising from safeguarding breaches and reputational risks arising from negative publicity.

Each entry should include the nature of the risk, the potential consequences, the existing controls in place and any further actions planned. Each risk should be assigned to an individual who is accountable for monitoring it and implementing mitigation.

Each item should be assigned a timescale for review. The register should be reviewed at least annually, but higher-risk items may need quarterly or even monthly scrutiny. New risks should be added as circumstances change, and completed actions should be dated so that progress can be demonstrated. Over time, the register provides an audit trail of how risks have been identified, assessed and managed, which is valuable evidence of good governance in the eyes of regulators, funders and auditors. The table below gives an example of a risk register entry for a specific hazard.

Hazard	Uneven flooring in reception
Who might be harmed	Visitors and volunteers
Risk description	Trips and falls
Current controls in place	Area is signposted, and staff advise visitors
Risk level (low/med/high)	Medium
Additional actions needed	Arrange repair or install temporary floor mat
Person responsible	Facilities volunteer
Deadline	30/07/2025

Risk assessments

A risk assessment is a standardised method of identifying what might go wrong and taking sensible steps to prevent or minimise harm. The Health and Safety Executive defines a risk assessment as 'a careful examination of what, in your work, could harm people. It helps you decide whether you have done enough to prevent anyone coming to harm, or need to do more.'[71]

Risk assessments help organisations meet their legal duties under UK law, particularly those around health and safety, safeguarding and data protection. Risk assessments are designed to protect people and avoid preventable disruptions to services. If you employ five or more people, the Management of Health and Safety at Work Regulations 1999 require you to record your risk assessments.[72]

A risk assessment involves a few simple steps.

Identify the hazards

Carefully analyse each area of your business, not just the physical premises (eg financial, staffing, reputation and so on) and think about what could go wrong.

Identify who might be harmed and how

Think about whether and how any volunteers, employees, contractors or members of the public might be harmed, bearing in mind that vulnerable people, eg under-18s and people with disabilities, might be at greater risk of harm.

Evaluate the risks

Determine how much harm the risk could cause and how likely that is to happen. Many assessors use a risk matrix, plotting probability versus potential harm, to give a numerical value to the risk. A score of 1 would relate to a low probability and low potential harm, while 5 would be a serious and urgent risk that should be dealt with immediately, as illustrated in the table below.

Probability			
HIGH	3	4	5
MEDIUM	2	3	4
LOW	1	2	3
	LOW	**MEDIUM**	**HIGH**

Potential harm

Decide on suitable preventative measures

It can be useful to use the acronym ERIC (eliminate, reduce, inform, control) to identify how you could remove or mitigate the risk:

- **Eliminate:** In the first instance you should attempt to eliminate the risk by removing it completely.

- **Reduce:** Appropriate modifications can reduce the probability or severity of many risks.

- **Inform:** It is critical that those potentially affected are informed of the potential hazard and trained on how to avoid it.

- **Control:** Control measures aim to reduce the probability of harm by using things like physical barriers, PPE (personal protective equipment) and safe working practices.

Insurance

Insurance is another way of mitigating risk, although it is not a replacement for good risk management procedures. Some insurances are compulsory or may be a requirement from funders or providers. The main types of insurance most likely to be relevant to your organisation are:

- **Employers' liability insurance** – a legal requirement if you employ anyone, even part-time or seasonally

- **Public liability insurance** – cover for injuries or damage to property caused by your activities; is compulsory if you have premises, deliver services or run events

- **Officer or trustee indemnity insurance** – cover for board members for legal costs or claims arising from their decisions, as long as they were made in good faith

- **Professional indemnity insurance** – required for organisations giving advice or providing advocacy services

- **Standalone event insurance** – for things like festivals, fundraisers, conferences or large public events

- **Cyber insurance** – increasingly popular with organisations, particularly those handling sensitive or financial data, but policies can contain significant exclusions so should be checked carefully to ensure they match your needs

Data protection

Managing data responsibly is both a legal obligation and a matter of trust. Not-for-profit organisations often hold sensitive information about volunteers, staff, supporters, members and service users. Data breaches can cause real harm to both the individuals concerned and to your organisation's credibility.

In the UK all organisations that collect personal data must comply with UK GDPR[73] and the Data Protection Act 2018[74] and register with the ICO.

Personal data is anything that can identify a living person, which includes names, addresses, contact details, opinions and photographs. Anonymised data, which has been processed to remove or alter identifying information, making it impossible to identify the individual, is not covered by data protection law.

The most common lawful bases for data processing are:

- **Consent** – where someone has actively agreed to their data being used

- **Legitimate interests** – where your use of the data is necessary and balanced

- **Contract** – where the data is needed to fulfil an agreement

You are required to provide clear privacy notices that explain what data you collect, why you collect it, how it will be used, how long it will be stored and how people can exercise their rights, including how to make a subject access request (SAR) and the right to be forgotten, ie have all data relating to them erased. These notices should be available at the point where you collect data, for example on forms or online sign-up pages.

Special category data

Special category data is a subset of personal data that is considered more sensitive and therefore requires a higher level of protection. Special category data is more likely to impact someone's rights and freedoms if it is misused or disclosed without proper safeguards.

The UK GDPR defines special category data as racial or ethnic origin, political opinions, religious or philosophical beliefs, trade union membership, genetic data and biometric data (where used for identification), and data concerning health, sex life or sexual orientation.[75] You must also be careful when collecting data that could allow inference of special category information, for example dietary requirements that may correlate to a religious belief or health condition.

Data storage

All data must be stored securely. It's important to use password-protected and encrypted systems and restrict access to only those who need it. You must avoid storing personal data in personal email inboxes or on unprotected USB sticks. If you use cloud-based systems, you must ensure they are hosted in countries with GDPR-compliant data protection standards, such as countries in the UK and EEA.

Everyone who handles data should understand their responsibilities and know how to respond to data breaches or SARs. Keep a record of their training and update it annually.

You are also required to have a data breach policy in place. This should outline what to do if data is lost, stolen or accessed without permission. The ICO must be notified within seventy-two hours of a serious breach, and individuals must be informed if their rights and freedoms are likely to be affected.

Key points

- **Risk management.** This is the process of identifying and assessing events or situations that could negatively affect your organisation and taking steps to reduce any risks. Everyone needs to be trained in risk management, but the ultimate responsibility lies with the board.

- **Risk assessments.** A risk assessment must be completed to assess every activity, including normal work activities, that could cause harm to anyone involved. Each risk assessment must recognise any potential hazards, identify who might be harmed and how, evaluate the risks and decide on suitable preventative measures.

- **Data protection.** Responsible data management is a vital component in the legal management of any not-for-profit. All organisations that collect personal data must comply with UK GDPR and the Data Protection Act 2018 and register with the ICO.

23

Data Management

Not-for-profit organisations handle a wide variety of sensitive and legally significant data, from donation records and accounts to personnel files and safeguarding disclosures. Retaining information for too long increases the risk of data breaches and non-compliance with the data protection laws covered in Chapter 22. Not retaining them for long enough can lead to penalties, missing audit trails, and poor governance.

Electronic data

Electronic data will make up the bulk of information held by a not-for-profit. Most data management policies include documents, spreadsheets, databases, financial and HR systems, websites and cloud-based storage.

However, many organisations overlook data held in their emails, social media accounts, messaging apps and shared calendars.

One of the challenges with electronic data is its tendency to proliferate. Multiple versions of the same file may exist across different devices, and attachments can be kept in inboxes long after they are relevant.

Email management

Email remains one of the biggest sources of unmanaged data in not-for-profits. A good email-management plan should include clear expectations for staff and volunteers about what should and should not be kept in their inboxes and how to spot and remove duplicates. Policies might require that important correspondence is saved into shared folders or case management systems and that routine emails are deleted after a set period. Organisations should consider setting automatic retention rules, such as archiving or deleting emails after a defined number of years.

A good plan will also cover how to handle attachments and sensitive information. For example, large or sensitive documents should be shared through secure cloud platforms with access controls, rather than as email attachments that can easily be forwarded outside the organisation. Policies should set out when encryption or password protection is required, and how staff should deal with personal data sent to them by email.

Filing conventions

Establishing a consistent digital filing structure can save hours of time as well as helping you comply with your data protection responsibilities. To minimise the risk of information being shared incorrectly and allow the correct data policies to be applied, it is best practice to:

- Use standardised folder names

- Agree file naming conventions

- Ensure everyone at your organisation saves documents in shared spaces rather than on personal devices

I recommend numbering your high-level folders (eg 01 Admin, 02 Finance, 03 Website) so your front page is not cluttered and the folders remain in the same order, even when new folders are added. This system means you don't have to guess how someone else categorised the information (eg finance, accounts, current year and so on). Folders within each of the high-level folders can also be numbered; for example, in the finance folder you might have 01 Year end, 02 Bank reconciliation, 03 Donors and 04 Gift Aid.

It is best to name individual files with the date of creation at the beginning of their name, with the year first, followed by the month and then the day. File names should also clearly indicate what each file relates to.

Dating files in this way allows you to quickly identify the latest version of a file as well as making it easy to implement your data retention policy.

Document retention, archiving and destruction

Different types of records have different retention requirements. Some are guided by law, others by best practice or funder requirements.

The ICO guidance on retention and destruction of information[76] and collecting and keeping employment records[77] recommends developing a retention policy that records:

- The types of records held

- The purpose of each record

- The retention period

- Instructions on how to dispose of the information

The policy should also reflect your legal obligations, business needs and best practice.

Employment records

For employment records, you need to be aware that different types of data have different retention rules both during and after employment, and your policy should be 'reasonable'. For example, keeping records of verbal warnings after they have expired may be seen as unreasonable.

Records of unsuccessful applications should be kept for up to twelve months. Employment records should generally be retained for six years after employment ends, to allow for potential contractual or discrimination claims, as stipulated in the Limitation Act 1980.[78] There is an exception under the COSHH Regulations 2002, with records relating to serious incidents such as disease and exposure to harmful substances needing to be retained for at least forty years.[79]

Financial records

Financial records have a minimum retention period of three tax years for a private company and six tax years for a public company, under the Companies Act 2006.[80] However, VAT legislation requires records are kept for at least six years.[81]

Best practice dictates keeping records for seven – referred to as *six plus one* – years to allow for overlapping financial years and delays in the reporting periods.

Safeguarding records

NSPCC guidance recommends keeping child protection records until the child turns twenty-five (thirty in Northern Ireland).[82] For adult safeguarding, it is generally accepted that records should be kept for at least seven years after the case is closed, to support any future investigations or legal action.

Health and safety records

For health and safety records there are different guidelines for different types of record. RIDDOR regulations require accident reports to be retained for three years from the date of the incident.[83]

There is no set amount of time for which risk assessments must be retained. Best practice is generally to keep the risk assessment for as long as it remains relevant to the task or activity or is superseded by a new risk assessment.[84]

Governing documents

Governing documents should be retained in perpetuity, as they are essential for historical and legal continuity.[85]

The governing documents are the rules your organisation has to abide by and include records of changes to directors, trustees and the registered office. This may be your constitution, articles of association, trust deed or Royal Charter, depending on how your organisation was formed. If your organisation has changed form, for example by becoming incorporated or achieving charitable status, you will have more than one type of governing document. You may also have multiple versions of the documents, showing the progression of the organisation over the years.

Minutes

Minutes – both board minutes and AGM/EGM minutes, with the accompanying resolutions – are the legal record of decisions and the reasoning behind them.

There is some conflict in the guidance on how long to keep minutes. Company law states that minutes must be kept for at least ten years,[86] while Charity Commission guidance for unincorporated charities and trusts is at least six years.[87] A report by the British Academy Research Group in partnership with the Charity Finance Group, published in 2017, notes that minutes provide evidence of both governance and the development of an organisation and should, therefore, be kept permanently.[88] This is supported by 2019 guidance from the National Archives.[89] Your organisation must set and follow an appropriate retention policy, bearing in mind the relevant legislation.

Insurance documents

The recommended retention period for general insurance documents is six to twelve years after the end of the policy, to retain cover for claims relating to incidents that happened during the period.[90] This allows six years to bring a claim and then the time any legal process takes after this.

The 2008 amendment to regulations around employers' liability means that outdated insurance certificates no longer need to be retained.[91] However, due to the potential of long-tail claims, where the 'harm' caused through employment is not evident until many years later, such as in the case of asbestos-related health claims, I recommend you keep certificates on record for as long as practicably possible.

Fundraising and donor records

Donation records and Gift Aid certificates should be retained for a minimum of six years after the last donation. In practice, this becomes seven years for the relevant financial records. If the donor has consented to receive marketing communications, the ICO recommends refreshing this consent every two years.[92]

Example retention schedule

To avoid confusion, it is advisable to maintain a retention schedule listing all the records you keep and the retention period for each one. See the table below for an example of this list.

Type of document	Retention period	Legal/best practice basis
Annual accounts, receipts	Documents covering 3 full financial years of data for a private, non-VAT-registered company	Companies Act 2006
	At least 6 full financial years for a VAT-registered company	HMRC VAT Notice 700/21
Contracts (staff/ services)	6 years post-end of contract	Limitation Act 1980
Personnel files	6 years post-employment	Employment claims limit
	Exception for records relating to serious disease or exposure to harmful substances which is at least 40 years	COSHH Regulations 2002
Volunteer records	3 years post-volunteering	Good practice
Safeguarding cases	Up to age 25 (child) At least 7 years (adult)	NSPCC/local authority guidance

Type of document	Retention period	Legal/best practice basis
Accident reports	Adults 3 years	RIDDOR, Limitation Act 1980
Risk assessments	As long as the risk assessment remains relevant or until superseded	Good practice
Insurance documents	6–12 years	Limitation Act 1980
Employers' liability insurance documents	40 years	Recommended in case of long-tail liability claims
Governing documents	Permanently	Good practice
Donor and fundraising data	6 financial years after the last donation	HMRC, GDPR

Archiving and destruction

Once the retention period ends, records should either be archived or securely destroyed. It is vital to remember that you should archive only information that holds genuine historical, legal or governance value. You must not retain information just in case you ever need it again, because keeping data longer than necessary is a breach of UK GDPR.

Paper records can be destroyed either onsite, using an appropriate crosscut shredder; or offsite, by employing a specialist confidential waste service.

Electronic records, including emails, attachments and data stored in backups, needs to be permanently deleted from IT systems. You may not need to edit past backups, but you should ensure that deleted files are not restored and that backup sets are deleted at the end of their retention period.

It is also important to train staff and volunteers in good email practice and to use automatic expiry tools and retention tools where possible.

Key points

- **Email management.** A lot of data is received, stored and transmitted via email. A good email-management policy will reduce proliferation, ensure important information is captured and comply with data security requirements.

- **Filing systems.** Storing all your files and records in a systematic way not only makes it easier to retrieve information; it also reduces errors and helps you to maintain compliance with data protection requirements.

- **Record retention.** Each type of record, certificate and policy has an ideal retention period, either required by law or recommended by best practice. Your retention schedule should list how long each type of record used by your organisation needs to be kept.

- **Archiving and destruction.** After any retention period expires, records must be securely destroyed, or archived only if that doesn't break data protection rules regarding any particular file or document.

24

Monitoring, Evaluation And Strategic Review

It is essential that you understand whether your not-for-profit organisation is making a difference and can evaluate its impact. Monitoring and evaluation – often referred to as M&E – helps you understand what is and isn't working and why.

This chapter explores how to build monitoring and evaluation into your everyday practice, how to define and measure impact and how to report meaningfully to those who support and benefit from your work. We then look at the process of strategic review, and how you can use the results from your monitoring and evaluation to plan your next evolution in a constant process of learning and adapting, in response to both internal and external factors.

Review, reflection and renewal are related but distinct processes. When used together, they provide a powerful cycle of learning and development. Each serves a different purpose, employs different methods and is best suited to particular moments in your organisation's journey.

Tools and approaches for monitoring and evaluation

There are many ways to collect monitoring and evaluation data, and the right tools depend on your goals, resources and audience.

Monitoring is the process of collecting the data about your activities. It could include tracking numerical outputs (like how many people attended a session) and qualitative outcomes (like changes in knowledge, confidence or behaviour).

Evaluation is the process of analysing the data to work out whether your work is effective, relevant and impactful. It might involve basic comparisons, identifying themes in feedback or tracking trends over time. You will need to check whether there are any emerging trends or results that surprised you, and how those compare with what you expected. You will also measure whether you met your goals and, if not, look at specific areas that fell short.

Impact is the broader, longer-term change your organisation contributes to. It can be hard to measure directly, but you can build a picture using evidence, stories and learning. You should avoid overclaiming or assuming causation when the data shows only a correlation.

Review

At the beginning of any review process, it is important to think about what information you want to collect so it can be built into the right stages of the process. This includes thinking about what you will need for internal learning and what your external stakeholders will expect to see. You can then balance this with the methods that your audience will find most empowering and respectful.

At the beginning of a project, you should define the outcomes you want so you can devise a way of measuring whether or not they been achieved. This means identifying indicators that will measure progress and building in methods for collecting the data. For example, an indicator for reduced loneliness might be the number of people attending social events, or how often participants report feeling connected. Indicators should be specific, measurable (quantitatively or qualitatively) and relevant to your activities.

It is vital to collect data ethically. Explain why you are requesting the information, how it will be used and how privacy will be protected. Participation should be voluntary, and you should avoid collecting more data than you need. Involving the people you support in designing your evaluation approach, sometimes called *participatory evaluation*, can improve relevance and accountability.

Here are some useful ways data can be collected:

- **Sign-up information.** If you are running events, registration or sign-in forms will help you track participation. This data can show not just how many people attended but whether they are returning or new participants. Designing specific questions to be asked during the sign-up process could allow you to obtain information about demographics and accessibility requirements.

- **Surveys.** Surveys and questionnaires are useful for collecting structured feedback. They might be paper-based or electronic, completed in person or online. It can be useful to use a mixture of questions with a numerical scale, for example 1–5 for levels of satisfaction, and include open questions for comments. Numerical answers are much easier to analyse and present graphically, but comments can give you qualitative feedback. Pre- and post-surveys can demonstrate a change over time and are particularly valuable when measuring the impact on individuals.

- **Interviews and focus groups.** These allow for richer, more nuanced insights. Interviews and focus groups are often led by experienced facilitators and can be particularly helpful when exploring complex experiences, identifying unintended effects or shaping future services.

- **Observations or activity logs.** These record events that happen during the delivery phase. They are useful for tracking engagement levels, identifying common issues or supporting reflection.

- **Case studies.** These are created after the project ends, often with insight from the data analysis, to provide detailed stories of individuals or communities who have benefited from the organisation's work. They are particularly valuable when used in reports or future funding applications to bring the numbers to life, particularly in small-scale or relationship-based work.

Creating a culture of reflection and renewal

A culture of reflection and renewal requires organisations to value learning and to view mistakes as opportunities for growth.

Reflection

Reflection brings in the human experience and creates space for growth and learning. Methods that support good reflection include:

- Learning debriefs after events or campaigns

- Team or board away days

- Appreciative enquiry – exploring what went well

- Critical incident analysis – unpacking what went wrong

- Individual journaling or regular reflective supervision

Creating a reflective culture requires confident leadership and leaders modelling good behaviours. Reflection should happen at every level, including leadership meetings, frontline teams, volunteer groups and partnership forums.

This might mean building in space at the end of meetings for learning points. It could involve regular check-ins where people can say what's gone well, what's been hard and what they have learned. It might also mean holding quarterly 'pause days', where the team reflect on the big picture.

Renewal

Renewal is where the insights from evaluation and reflection feed into strategy and change. A good strategic plan:

- Builds on the organisation's strengths

- Addresses its challenges

- Aligns with the needs of its audience

- Is ambitious but achievable

- Is flexible enough to respond to change

Creating a strategic plan could mean updating your mission, reshaping your services or just re-energising your team.

Renewal often comes after the end of a funding period, due to a change in leadership or during a post-crisis recovery.

Conducting a strategic review

A strategic review is a structured assessment of your organisation's current position and future direction. It needs both data and emotion, using the numbers from evaluation and the insights from reflection.

Benefits

A good strategic review will help you:

- Understand your impact and environment
- Focus your energy and resources
- Make decisions with confidence
- Engage your team and stakeholders
- Stay true to your mission in changing times

A good review will uncover a lot of information. It can be helpful to group your findings into themes such as impact and relevance, capacity and resources, risks and resilience, and opportunities and innovation. Look for patterns, contradictions and 'aha!' moments.

A strategic review should lead to clear choices and an obvious course of action. You might decide to refresh your mission, shift focus to certain services, close or pause some activities or explore new partnerships or funding models

The strategic review process

The process should be led by the board, who provide oversight and big-picture thinking. Staff and volunteers can give operational insight and ideas, while involving service users or beneficiaries will keep the review grounded in lived experience. Where appropriate, you should involve partners or funders to test your assumptions.

Write a simple purpose statement for the review, for example: *By [month], we want to understand our current position and options so we can make confident decisions about our future strategy.*

Plan the process but keep it proportionate. A two- to three-month timeline often works well, with clear checkpoints and updates to your board or steering group. You should decide:

- Who will lead it – a trustee, staff lead or external facilitator

- Who will be involved – board, staff, volunteers, service users

- What methods you will use

- What decisions the review is intended to inform

Look at both internal and external factors, including current results, resources, societal trends, legislation, partners and competitors. Tools like a simple SWOT (strengths, weaknesses, opportunities, threats) analysis[93] or Theory of Change (ToC)[94] can help structure this.

A SWOT is diagnostic and helps you examine your current internal and external environment. By contrast, a ToC asks you to define a long-term change you want to see, then map backwards through the intermediate outcomes, activities and assumptions needed to get there.

Reflect on your goals and strategy, then plan how your resources and activities will lead to the desired outcomes under certain assumptions to form a logical roadmap for change. A ToC can be expressed as a narrative or visual change map, capturing both the *why* and the *how* of your change plan, and is a valuable tool for explaining your vision to internal and external stakeholders.

Write up a short strategic review summary (two or three pages is plenty), including:

- Your key insights

- The options considered

- Your recommendations

- Next steps and timescales

This summary will become the foundation for the strategic planning process, or the basis for discussion at your next board meeting or away day.

Key points

- **Review.** Ethically collected data will allow you to understand the effectiveness, relevance and impact of your organisation. When the review process is combined with reflection and renewal, a powerful cycle of learning and development can be created.

- **Reflection.** Reflection creates space for learning at all levels, using approaches like debriefs, critical incident analysis, appreciative enquiry and journaling.

- **Renewal.** Renewal uses insights from reflection and evaluation to inform strategy, strengthen services and re-energise the team.

- **Strategic review.** Using the numbers from evaluation and the insights from reflection, the strategic review will help you understand your organisation's current position and what you need to do to optimise your future direction and stay aligned with your mission.

Conclusion

As you reach the final pages of this book, take a moment to reflect on your journey. I hope you now have a deeper understanding of why you have to do certain tasks and what it means to run a not-for-profit organisation in the UK.

Part One explored the rules that define a not-for-profit and the structural foundations of any well-governed organisation, identifying the different legal forms and how to choose the right one for your organisation. We noted the importance of the governing document, the duties of directors and trustees, and how the law dictates their responsibilities. Finally, we delved into some of the history behind the laws and agencies that govern not-for-profit organisations in the UK.

Part Two looked at the different roles of people within the organisation, whether volunteers, staff or contractors. We learned why volunteers are treated differently to staff and how to recruit and support them without conferring employment rights. The essentials of becoming an employer were covered, from contracts and pensions to supervision and staff wellbeing. We considered how to create inclusive cultures, handle conflict constructively and embed safeguarding in day-to-day practice.

Part Three looked at the day-to-day activities of organisations, including the many ways organisations build relationships with their wider community. Whether through formal membership models or service delivery, we saw how to design for accessibility, accountability and relevance. This part introduced event planning, different approaches to collaboration, and the differences between advocacy and campaigning. Finally, we looked at fundraising and organisational grant funding, including where grant money comes from and how it is distributed.

Part Four looked at the responsibilities of the board with regard to governance and how ethical leadership and decision making underpin success and sustainability. Managing finance and budgets is a large part of the board's responsibility, so I introduced some of the terminology and basic budgeting theories. Risk and data management are an important part of this section, as is understanding the legal basis for document retention and destruction. This part concluded with tips on how to monitor and evaluate the organisation's impact and how to create a culture of reflection, including guidance on undertaking a strategic review to inform your organisation's next evolution.

With all this knowledge, I trust you now feel more confident in your role and understand how the different parts of a not-for-profit organisation connect. While most of the topics in this book would need whole books of their own to cover them in depth, you will now have a good understanding of all the areas you need to consider. Remember, you don't have to know everything, and you don't have to do everything alone. The not-for-profit sector is built on collaboration, generosity and shared learning. There are countless infrastructure bodies, funders, networks, helplines and peers who are ready to walk alongside you.

As you move forward in managing and improving your organisation, remember to take every opportunity to celebrate. Celebrate the small wins and the major successes. Tell everyone what you do and why you do it. You never know, there may just be a new donor or trustee looking on with interest.

Before you close this book, I would like to invite you to join my community to continue your learning and network with your peers in the not-for-profit space. Further information can be found at www.notforprofitknowhow .co.uk, and you can connect with me at www.linkedin .com/in/kirstieyork.

Notes

1. Charity Commission, *Charity Commission Annual Report and Accounts 2024 to 2025* (GOV.UK, 9 July 2025), www.gov.uk /government/publications/charity-commission-annual -report-and-accounts-2024-to-2025/charity-commission -annual-report-and-accounts-2024-to-2025, accessed 28 August 2025
2. Charity Commission, 'Charitable Purposes' (GOV.UK, 16 September 2013), www.gov.uk/government/publications /charitable-purposes/charitable-purposes, accessed 1 September 2025
3. Charities and Trustee Investment (Scotland) Act 2005 (2005 asp 10, explanatory notes), www.legislation.gov.uk/asp/2005/10 /notes, accessed 1 September 2025
4. Charities Act (Northern Ireland) 2008 (2008 c 12, part 14, section 180), www.legislation.gov.uk/nia/2008/12/section /180, accessed 7 September 2025
5. Charity Commission, 'How to register a charity (CC21b)' (GOV. UK, 21 May 2014, updated 2 February 2015), www.gov.uk /guidance/how-to-register-your-charity-cc21b, accessed 15 May 2025
6. HM Revenue and Customs, 'Read the Community Amateur Sports Clubs: Detailed guidance notes' (GOV.UK, updated 9 September 2025), www.gov.uk/government/publications /community-amateur-sports-clubs-detailed-guidance

-notes/community-amateur-sports-clubs-detailed-guidance
-notes, accessed 15 September 2025

7. Sport England, 'National governing bodies' (no date), www
.sportengland.org/guidance-and-support/national
-governing-bodies?section=recognised-ngbs-section,
accessed 15 September 2025

8. UK Government, 'Register as a community amateur sports
club (CASC)' (GOV.UK, no date), www.gov.uk/register
-a-community-amateur-sports-club/eligibility, accessed 15
May 2025

9. Companies House, 'Companies House confirms identity
verification rollout from 18 November 2025' (GOV.UK, 5
August 2025), www.gov.uk/government/news/companies
-house-confirms-identity-verification-rollout-from-18
-november-2025, accessed 29 August 2025

10. Companies House, 'Model articles of association for limited
companies' (GOV.UK, 21 November 2014, updated 10
October 2017), www.gov.uk/guidance/model-articles-of
-association-for-limited-companies, accessed 15 September
2025

11. Record of Charters Granted, https://privycouncil.independent
.gov.uk/wp-content/uploads/2025/05/2025-05-13-Record-of
-Charters-Granted.pdf, accessed 24 September 2025

12. Charity Commission, 'Charitable purposes' (GOV.UK, 16
September 2013), www.gov.uk/government/publications
/charitable-purposes/charitable-purposes, accessed 15 May
2025

13. Charity Commission, 'Public benefit: Rules for charities' (GOV.
UK, 14 February 2014), www.gov.uk/guidance/public
-benefit-rules-for-charities, accessed 3 September 2025

14. Charity Commission, 'Setting up a charity: Model governing
documents' (GOV.UK, 1 January 2012, updated 11 October
2022), www.gov.uk/government/publications/setting
-up-a-charity-model-governing-documents, accessed 7
September 2025

15. Charity Commission, 'Exempt charities (CC23)' (GOV.
UK, updated 14 June 2023), www.gov.uk/government
/publications/exempt-charities-cc23/exempt-charities,
accessed 15 May 2025

16. Charity Commission, 'Excepted charities' (GOV.UK, 11 June
2014), www.gov.uk/government/publications/excepted
-charities/excepted-charities--2, accessed 15 May 2025

17. Credas, 'A timeline of Companies House' (Credas, 27 April 2023, updated 27 March 2025), https://credas.com/news /a-timeline-of-companies-house, accessed 2 September 2025

18. Companies House and Department for Business and Trade, 'Companies House celebrates 10 years of open data' (GOV.UK, 22 June 2025), www.gov.uk/government /news/companies-house-celebrates-10-years-of-open-data, accessed 16 September 2025

19. Companies House, 'Companies House approach to financial penalties' (GOV.UK, 27 September 2024), www.gov.uk /government/publications/companies-house-approach-to -financial-penalties, accessed 15 May 2025

20. Companies Act 2006, www.legislation.gov.uk/ukpga/2006/46 /section/388, accessed 31 May 2025

21. Charity Commission, *Charity Commission Annual Report and Accounts 2024 to 2025* (GOV.UK, 9 July 2025), www.gov.uk /government/publications/charity-commission-annual -report-and-accounts-2024-to-2025/charity-commission -annual-report-and-accounts-2024-to-2025, accessed 3 September 2025

22. OSCR, 'Who we are' (OSCR, no date), www.oscr.org.uk/about -oscr/who-we-are, accessed 2 September 2025

23. CCNI, *Annual Report and Accounts 2024–25* (The Charity Commission for Northern Ireland, 2025), www .charitycommissionni.org.uk/about-us/about-the-charity -commission/annual-reports-and-accounts, accessed 2 September 2025

24. The Privy Council, https://privycouncil.independent.gov.uk /the-privy-council, accessed 24 September 2025

25. Record of Charters Granted, https://privycouncil .independent.gov.uk/wp-content/uploads/2025/05/2025-05 -13-Record-of-Charters-Granted.pdf, accessed 24 September 2025

26. Charity Governance Code, 'Good governance' (Charity Governance Code Steering Group, no date), www .charitygovernancecode.org, accessed 2 September 2025

27. NCVO, 'Individual trustee performance reviews', www.ncvo .org.uk/help-and-guidance/governance/board-basics/tools -and-guidance/individual-trustee-performance-reviews, accessed 25 September 2025

28. Health and Safety at Work etc. Act 1974, www.legislation.gov
    .uk/ukpga/1974/37/contents, accessed 8 September 2025
29. Equality Act 2010, www.legislation.gov.uk/ukpga/2010/15
    /contents, accessed 16 September 2025
30. NCVO, 'If volunteering goes wrong' (National Council for
    Voluntary Organisations, no date), www.ncvo.org.uk
    /get-involved/volunteering/if-volunteering-goes-wrong,
    accessed 2 September 2025
31. NCVO, 'Key findings from Time Well Spent 2023' (National
    Council for Voluntary Organisations, 1 May 2023), www
    .ncvo.org.uk/news-and-insights/news-index/key-findings
    -from-time-well-spent-2023, accessed 18 May 25
32. NCVO, 'Solving volunteer problems' (last reviewed 12 April
    2021), www.ncvo.org.uk/help-and-guidance/involving
    -volunteers/supporting-and-managing-volunteers/solving
    -volunteer-problems, accessed 29 October 2025
33. Equality Act 2010, www.legislation.gov.uk/ukpga/2010/15
    /contents, accessed 8 September 2025
34. UK Government, 'Disciplinary procedures and action against
    you at work' (GOV.UK, no date), www.gov.uk/disciplinary
    -procedures-and-action-at-work/how-disciplinary
    -procedures-work, accessed 14 August 2025
35. Acas, 'Code of Practice on disciplinary and grievance
    procedures' (Acas, 11 March 2015), www.acas.org.uk
    /acas-code-of-practice-on-disciplinary-and-grievance
    -procedures/html, accessed 14 August 2025
36. HSE, 'Work-related stress and how to manage it' (Health and
    Safety Executive, no date), www.hse.gov.uk/stress/risk
    -assessment.htm, accessed 18 September 2025
37. Acas, 'Acas Code of Practice on disciplinary and grievance
    procedures' (Acas, 11 March 2015), www.acas.org.uk
    /acas-code-of-practice-on-disciplinary-and-grievance
    -procedures/html, accessed 2 September 2025
38. NCVO, 'If volunteering goes wrong' (National Council for
    Voluntary Organisations, no date), www.ncvo.org.uk
    /get-involved/volunteering/if-volunteering-goes-wrong,
    accessed 2 September 2025
39. HM Revenue & Customs, 'Check employment status for tax'
    (GOV.UK, 2 March 2017, updated 30 April 2025), www.gov
    .uk/guidance/check-employment-status-for-tax, accessed
    18 September 2025

40. Equality Act 2010, www.legislation.gov.uk/ukpga/2010/15 /contents, accessed 8 September 2025
41. Disability Discrimination Act 1995, www.legislation.gov.uk /ukpga/1995/50/contents, accessed 8 September 2025
42. WC3, 'Web Content Accessibility Guidelines (WCAG) 2.2' (World Wide Web Consortium, 12 December 2024), www .w3.org/TR/WCAG22, accessed 26 May 2025
43. The Public Sector Bodies (Websites and Mobile Applications) (No 2) Accessibility Regulations 2018, www.legislation.gov .uk/uksi/2018/952/contents, accessed 26 May 2025
44. Partnership Act 1890, www.legislation.gov.uk/ukpga/Vict/53 -54/39/introduction, accessed 28 May 2025
45. Human Rights Act 1998, www.legislation.gov.uk/ukpga/1998 /42/contents, accessed 28 May 2025
46. Public Order Act 1986, www.legislation.gov.uk/ukpga/1986 /64/contents, accessed 28 May 2025
47. Charity Commission, 'Campaigning and political activity guidance for charities (CC9)' (GOV.UK, 1 March 2008, updated 7 November 2022), www.gov.uk/government /publications/speaking-out-guidance-on-campaigning-and -political-activity-by-charities-cc9, accessed 15 May 2025
48. Transparency of Lobbying, Non-Party Campaigning and Trade Union Administration Act 2014, www.legislation.gov .uk/ukpga/2014/4/contents, accessed 28 May 2025
49. Charity Commission, 'Charity fundraising: A guide to trustee duties' (GOV.UK, updated 31 October 2022), www.gov.uk /government/publications/charities-and-fundraising-cc20 /charities-and-fundraising, accessed 30 May 2025
50. Fundraising Regulator, 'Code of Fundraising Practice' (Fundraising Regulator, no date), www .fundraisingregulator.org.uk/code, accessed 30 May 2025
51. Licensing Act 2003, www.legislation.gov.uk/ukpga/2003/17 /contents, accessed 22 September 2025
52. Charities and Trustee Investment (Scotland) Act 2005, www .legislation.gov.uk/asp/2005/10/part/2, accessed 30 May 2025
53. Civic Government (Scotland) Act 1982, www.legislation.gov .uk/ukpga/1982/45/contents, accessed 22 May 2025
54. Charities Act (Northern Ireland) 2008, www.legislation.gov .uk/nia/2008/12/part/13, accessed 30 May 2025

55. Northern Ireland (Licensing (NI) Order 1996), www
    .legislation.gov.uk/nisi/1996/3158/contents/made, accessed
    22 September 2025
56. Street and House To House Collections Act 1962, www
    .legislation.ie/eli/1962/act/13/enacted/en/html, accessed
    22 September 2025
57. Gambling Act 2005, www.legislation.gov.uk/ukpga/2005/19
    /contents, accessed 30 May 2025
58. Gambling Commission, 'What we do' (Gambling Commission,
    no date), www.gamblingcommission.gov.uk/about-us,
    accessed 30 May 2025
59. Gambling Commission, 'Definition of a lottery' (Gambling
    Commission, no date), www.gamblingcommission.gov
    .uk/licensees-and-businesses/guide/page/definition-of
    -a-lottery, accessed 15 May 2025
60. Fundraising Regulator, *Code of Fundraising Practice 2025*, (2025),
    www.fundraisingregulator.org.uk/sites/default/files
    /2025-09/Fundraising%20Regulator%20-%20Code%20of
    %20Fundraising%20Practice%20for%20amends%20V2.pdf,
    accessed 23 September 2025
61. The Charitable Collections (Transitional Provisions) Order
    1974 13, www.legislation.gov.uk/uksi/1974/140/pdfs/uksi
    _19740140_en.pdf, accessed 23 September 2025
62. Fundraising Regulator, *Code of Fundraising Practice 2025*, (2025),
    www.fundraisingregulator.org.uk/sites/default/files
    /2025-09/Fundraising %20Regulator%20-%20Code%20of
    %20Fundraising%20Practice%20for%20amends %20V2.pdf,
    accessed 23 September 2025
63. UK Government, 'How Inheritance Tax works: Thresholds,
    rules and allowances' (GOV.UK, no date), www.gov.uk
    /inheritance-tax/gifts-to-charity, accessed 15 May 2025
64. Charity Commission, 'Safeguarding and protecting people
    for charities and trustees' (GOV.UK, 6 December 2017,
    updated 1 June 2022), www.gov.uk/guidance/safeguarding
    -duties-for-charity-trustees, accessed 1 June 2025
65. OSCR, 'Safeguarding guidance' (Office of the Scottish
    Charity Regulator, 23 April 2025, updated 20 August 2025),
    www.oscr.org.uk/managing-a-charity/trustee-duties
    /safeguarding-guidance, accessed 1 June 2025
66. CCNI, 'Safeguarding resources' (CCNI, no date), www
    .charitycommissionni.org.uk/charity-essentials
    /safeguarding-resources, accessed 6 September 2025

67. Bribery Act 2010, www.legislation.gov.uk/ukpga/2010/23 /section/7, accessed 1 June 2025

68. Charity Commission, 'Managing charity finances' (GOV.UK, 2 November 2020), www.gov.uk/government/publications /managing-charity-assets-and-resources-cc25, accessed 2 September 2025

69. UK Government, 'VAT for charities' (GOV.UK, no date), www .gov.uk/vat-charities/what-qualifies-for-relief, accessed 6 September 2025

70. ISO, 'ISO 31000:2018(en) Risk Management – Guidelines' (International Organization for Standardization, no date), www.iso.org/obp/ui/#iso:std:iso:31000:ed-2:v1:en, accessed 10 August 2025

71. HSE, 'Risk assessment' (Health and Safety Executive, no date), www.hse.gov.uk/workplacetransport/management/risk .htm, accessed 1 June 2025

72. The Management of Health and Safety at Work Regulations 1999, www.legislation.gov.uk/uksi/1999/3242/regulation/3, accessed 1 June 2025

73. Regulation (EU) 2016/679 of the European Parliament and of the Council, www.legislation.gov.uk/eur/2016/679 /contents, accessed 31 May 2025

74. Data Protection Act 2018, www.legislation.gov.uk/ukpga/2018 /12/contents/enacted, accessed 31 May 2025

75. Department for Environment, Food & Rural Affairs, *Appropriate Policy Document: Special category personal data and criminal offence data* [policy paper] (GOV.UK, 14 June 2023), www.gov.uk/government/publications /defra-appropriate-policy-documents/appropriate-policy -document-special-category-personal-data-and-criminal -offence-data, accessed 6 September 2025

76. ICO, 'Retention and destruction of information' (ICO, no date), https://ico.org.uk/for-organisations/foi/freedom-of -information-and-environmental-information-regulations /retention-and-destruction-of-information, accessed 1 June 2025

77. ICO, 'Employment practices and data protection: Keeping employment records' (ICO, no date), https://ico.org.uk /for-organisations/uk-gdpr-guidance-and-resources /employment/employment-practices-and-data-protection -keeping-employment-records, accessed 1 June 2025

78. Limitation Act 1980, www.legislation.gov.uk/ukpga/1980/58 /contents, accessed 31 May 2025

79. COSHH Regulations 2002 Regulation 10(5)(a), Regulation 11(3), www.legislation.gov.uk/uksi/2002/2677/data.pdf, accessed 23 September 2025

80. Companies Act 2006, www.legislation.gov.uk/ukpga/2006/46 /section/388, accessed 31 May 2025

81. HMRC, 'Record keeping (VAT Notice 700/21)' (GOV.UK, 26 September 2013, updated 18 March 2024), www.gov.uk /guidance/record-keeping-for-vat-notice-70021, accessed 31 May 2025

82. NSPCC, 'Child protection records retention and storage guidelines' (NSPCC, September 2022), https://learning .nspcc.org.uk/media/3324/child-protection-records -retention-and-storage-guidelines_june_2023.pdf, accessed 31 May 2025

83. The Reporting of Injuries, Diseases and Dangerous Occurrences Regulations 2013, www.legislation.gov.uk /uksi/2013/1471/regulation/12, accessed 23 September 2025

84. British Safety Council, 'Risk assessments: What they are, why they're important and how to complete them' (BSC, no date), www.britsafe.org/training-and-learning /informational-resources/risk-assessments-what-they -are-why-they-re-important-and-how-to-complete-them, accessed 23 September 2025

85. Charity Commission for England and Wales, 'Rules for charity meetings CC48' (GOV.UK, updated 19 July 2024), www.gov.uk/government/publications/charities-and -meetings-cc48/charities-and-meetings, accessed 23 September 2025

86. Companies Act 2006, Section 248, www.legislation.gov.uk /ukpga/2006/46/section/248, accessed 23 September 2025

87. Charity Commission for England and Wales, 'Rules for charity meetings CC48' (GOV.UK, updated 19 July 2024), www.gov.uk/government/publications/charities-and -meetings-cc48/charities-and-meetings, accessed 23 September 2025

88. C Clements, *Records Management in Charities: A toolkit for improvement* (British Academy and Charity Finance Group, 2017), www.voluntarysectorarchives.org.uk/wp-content

/uploads/2017/06/records-management-in-charities-9.pdf, accessed 23 September 2025

89. The National Archives – Management Framework for Retention and Transfer Charity Records and Archives, https://cdn.nationalarchives.gov.uk/documents/archives /management-framework-for-retention-and-transfer.pdf, accessed 24 September 2025

90. Limitation Act 1980, www.legislation.gov.uk/ukpga/1980/58, accessed 31 May 2025

91. The Employers' Liability (Compulsory Insurance) (Amendment) Regulations 2008, www.legislation.gov.uk /uksi/2008/1765/note/made, accessed 24 September 2025

92. ICO, 'How should we obtain, record and manage consent?' (ICO, no date), https://ico.org.uk/for-organisations/uk -gdpr-guidance-and-resources/lawful-basis/consent/how -should-we-obtain-record-and-manage-consent, accessed 7 September 2025

93. NCVO, 'SWOT' (NCVO, no date), www.ncvo.org.uk/help-and -guidance/tools/swot, accessed 7 September 2025

94. NCVO, 'Theory of Change' (NCVO, no date), www.ncvo .org.uk/help-and-guidance/strategy-and-impact/strategy -and-business-planning/theory-of-change, accessed 7 September 2025

Acknowledgements

Particular thanks go to my great friends Jane Creese and Tracy Andrew who gave me my first opportunity to work with a not-for-profit organisation and taught me so much.

Thank you to Derek Cunningham, MBE, who I had the pleasure of working alongside for a time. It was his tireless twenty-year devotion to Worcestershire Disability Football Club that made it such a welcoming and inclusive space at the heart of its community.

Thank you to Lucy McCarraher for her never-ending patience, and to all the inspirational ladies in the ABOO writing circle, without whom this book would never have existed. I add to this the fabulous publishing team at Rethink Press who have expertly converted my manuscript into a book I'm proud to call my own.

I greatly appreciate my beta readers Tony Drury, John Field, Chloe York, Tracy Andrew, Alex Myers, Belle Tubman, Max Moss, Paul Gardner and Mary Collin for their invaluable insights and feedback.

Much love also goes to my family – Chloe York, Jamie York and John Field – for all the time I've not been able to spend with you during my writing journey and for your unwavering support of me and Cygnul.

The Author

Kirstie York is the CEO of Cygnul Limited, which offers complete remote office services to not-for-profits, charities and professional membership associations. Kirstie's mission is to support not-for-profits in balancing their passion-driven work with the day-to-day demands of operations and organisational structure.

Kirstie began her career as a secretary, first in the NHS and then moving to police admin. Like many secretaries, she became skilled at organising information, keeping accurate records and ensuring compliance.

What she loved most, though, was being the bridge between people and process – the person who could listen carefully, spot what was needed and turn ideas into action. When Kirstie moved into the not-for-profit world in 2011, it felt like a natural step, and she quickly found her feet, using those same skills to translate emotional, mission-led conversations into practical, achievable plans.

Cygnul was born in 2014 as an alternative to redundancy, and Kirstie took over the helm in 2018 on her colleague's retirement. She truly understands the juggling act of running an organisation, because she's lived it. Her business has evolved from two people to a thriving team, working with a diverse range of organisations across multiple disciplines.

Over the years Kirstie has seen a range of approaches and challenges unique to each sector. The terminology, aims and objectives, partner organisations and stakeholders may differ dramatically, but what never varies is the formal and legal administration requirements.

Her one-to-one mentoring has naturally evolved into short, practical training courses and a membership community designed to foster connections, shared learning and ongoing professional development within the sector.

🌐 www.notforprofitknowhow.co.uk

🌐 www.cygnul.co.uk

in www.linkedin.com/in/kirstieyork

⬤ www.facebook.com/profile/61576811232898

⬤ www.facebook.com/groups/756958892027644